European Real Estate Markets

European Real Estate Markets

José Luis Suárez
Professor of Financial Management
IESE Business School
Madrid, Spain

University of Navarra

First published 2009 by
PALGRAVE MACMILLAN

Palgrave Macmillan in the UK is an imprint of Macmillan Publishers Limited, registered in England, company number 785998, of Houndmills, Basingstoke, Hampshire RG21 6XS.

Palgrave Macmillan in the US is a division of St Martin's Press LLC, 175 Fifth Avenue, New York, NY 10010.

Palgrave Macmillan is the global academic imprint of the above companies and has companies and representatives throughout the world.

Palgrave® and Macmillan® are registered trademarks in the United States, the United Kingdom, Europe and other countries.

ISBN-13: 978–0–230–01316–2
ISBN-10: 0–230–01316–3

This book is printed on paper suitable for recycling and made from fully managed and sustained forest sources. Logging, pulping and manufacturing processes are expected to conform to the environmental regulations of the country of origin.

A catalogue record for this book is available from the British Library.

Library of Congress Cataloging-in-Publication Data
Suárez, José Luis, 1953–
   European real estate markets/Jos Luis Suárez.
      p. cm.
   Includes index.
   ISBN 978–0–230–01316–2 (alk. paper)
   1. Real estate business—Europe. 2. Real estate investment—Europe.
   3. Mortgage loans—Europe. I. Title.
HD586.S83 2008
332.63'24094—dc22

2008027562

10   9   8   7   6   5   4   3   2   1
18   17   16   15   14   13   12   11   10   09

Printed and bound in China

For my wife, Liliana, for her encouraging
and continuous support

The International Center for Financial Research

The CIIF (International Center for Financial Research) is an interdisciplinary institution with an international outlook and a focus on teaching and research in finance. It was created at the beginning of 1992 to channel the financial research interest of a multidisciplinary group of professors at the IESE Business School in Madrid and has established itself as a nucleus of study within the School's activities.

Fifteen years on, our chief objectives remain the same:

- To find answers to the questions that confront the owners and managers of finance companies and the financial directors of all kind of companies in the performance of their duties.
- To develop new tools for financial management.
- To study in depth the changes that occur in markets and their effects on the financial dimension of business activities.

All of these activities are programmed and carried out with the support of our sponsoring companies. Apart from providing vital financial assistance, our sponsors also help to define the CIIF's research projects, ensuring their practical relevance. These companies are: Aena, AT Kearney, Caja Madrid, Fundación Ramón Areces, Grupo Endesa, The Royal Bank of Scotland and Unión Fenosa.

http://www.iese.edu/ciif/

Contents

List of Figures

List of Tables

List of Abbreviations

AMF	*Autorité des marchés financiers* (financial market authorities, France)
BI	*Fiscale Beleggingsinstelling* (Dutch REIT)
BRIC/BRICs	Brazil, Russia, India and China
CDO	collateralized debt obligation
CDS	credit default swap
CEA	Comité Européen des Assurances
CEBS	Committee of European Banking Supervision
CEE	Central and Eastern Europe
CMBS	commercial mortgage-backed securities
CRD	Capital Requirement Directive
EBIT	earnings before interest and taxes
EMFA	European Mortgage Finance Agency
EMU	European Monetary Union
EPRA	European Public Real Estate Association
EU	European Union
euribor	Euro Interbank Offered Rate
FBS	*Fundierte Bankschuldverschreibungen* (Austrian covered bonds)
FCP	*Fonds Commun de Placement* (Luxembourg real estate investment fund)
FIIs	*Fondi di investimento immobiliare* (Italian investment funds in immovable assets)
FIIs	*Fondos de Inversión Inmobiliaria* (Spanish investment funds in immovable assets)
FPI	*Fonds de placement immobilier* (France; alternative name for an RFA)
FSA	Financial Services Authority (UK)
FTSE	Financial Times Stock Exchange (London)
GAV	gross asset value
GDP	gross domestic product
GLA	gross leasable area
GOE	German open-ended fund
G-REIT	German REIT
GSE	government-sponsored enterprise (USA – e.g. Fannie Mae. Freddie Mac)
HBOS	Halifax Bank of Scotland (banking group)

HPI	Halifax House Price Index (UK)
ICSC	International Council of Shopping Centers
IFs	*Offene Immobilienfonds* (German investment funds in immovable assets)
IIFs	*Immobilien Investmentfonds* (Austrian investment funds in immovable assets)
INREV	European Association of Investors in Non-Listed Real Estate Vehicles
IPD	Investment Property Databank
J-REIT	Japanese REIT
libor	London Interbank Offered Rate
LPT	limited property trust (Australia)
MBS	mortgage-backed security
MFT	mutual fund trust (Canada)
MTN	medium-term note
NAREIT	National Association of Real Estate Investment Trusts
NCREIF	National Council of Real Estate Investment Fiduciaries (USA)
OPCI	*Organismes de Placement Collectif Immobilier* (French legal structure for real estate investment; replacement for SCPI)
PUT	property unit trust (South Africa)
RFA	*Règle de fonctionnement allégé* (French; type of OPCI), also called FPI (*Fonds de placement immobilier*)
REIC	real estate investment company (Korea)
REIF	former real estate fund regime in Italy (see SIIQ)
REIT	real estate investment trust
RMBS	residential mortgage-backed securities
SCF	*Société de Crédit Foncier* (France)
SCPI	*Société civile de placement immobilier* (French legal structure for real estate investment)
SGR	*Società di gestione del risparmio* (Italian management company for FIIs)
SICAFI	*Société d'investissement à capital fixe en immobilière* (Belgian REIT)
SICAV/SICAF	*Société d'investissement à capital variable/fixe* (Luxembourg REIT) (SICAV also in France)
SIFMA	Securities Industry and Financial Markets Association
SIIs	*Sociedades de Inversión Inmobiliaria* (Spanish real estate investment company)
SIIC	*Société d'investissement immobilier cotée* (French REIT)

SIIQ   *Società d'Intermediazone Quotate* (Italian REIT)
SIV   structured investment vehicle
SPPICV   *Société de placement à prépondérante immobilière*
            à capital variable (France; a type of OPCI)
SPV   special purpose vehicle
S_REIT   Singapore REIT
UCI   undertaking for collective investment
UCIT   Undertaking for the Collective Investment of
            Transferable Securities Directive
UK REIT   British REIT
ZWEX   Swiss residential market index

Introduction

Real estate activity, in general, is one of the mainstays of modern society. Virtually all human activities are performed in buildings that are the subject of planning and intervention by public authorities, and trade by private companies. At the level of individual households, in addition to the shelter provided by a dwelling, it usually comprises a significant part of personal wealth, and other assets may depend to a great extent on the health of the property markets, either through direct investment or via real estate funds, firms or pension funds.

The property sector also has an impact on the activity of financial institutions. One has only to look at what happened on the financial markets in the second half of 2007 and during the early months of 2008 to realize this. The financial turmoil current at the time of writing has been triggered by a types of mortgage loans existing in the USA known as 'subprime mortgages'. In fact, a large part of financial institutions' balance sheets (more than two-thirds in some European countries) is made up of mortgage loans, which have experienced very significant growth throughout the world in recent years, including in certain countries that have been long-standing members of the European Union (EU). A similar growth is now expected in the countries that have recently joined the EU. What happens on the property markets will continue to have a profound impact on the conditions and profitability of financial institutions' operations.

The real estate industry is also contributing to the activities of the financial markets in new senses. The real estate derivatives market is one example. Although the derivatives on property assets are a recent creation, they are experiencing strong growth in both volume and the number of countries in which they are traded. In the future, they may play a significant role in the management of real estate investment risk.

Property-based securities include mortgage bonds, a more traditional product whose issuance volume has also increased considerably, and the newer mortgage-backed securities (MBS). The MBS market has opened a new business area for financial operators, and a very opportune and necessary source of funding for financial institutions engaged in mortgage lending. The financial markets have gone a step further in developing this product, embedding the MBS in another tier of securities, the so-called collateralized debt obligations (CDOs), thereby further increasing the liquidity of assets – mortgage loans – that are basically illiquid.

1

The rapid growth of the new securities, and their complexity, have led many investors to take positions that they did not fully understand, with risk management systems that did not cover all possible scenarios. Because of this, ascertaining the full impact that the lower quality of certain assets has had on investor portfolios is a very slow and painful process. Many financial institutions that had made provision for losses on the deterioration of assets after the summer of 2007 have had to revise their balance sheets further downwards.

Another important aspect of the situation at the time of writing is the increasingly global nature of the property markets. One visible sign of this growing globalization is the increase – year on year – of cross-country investment, as will be seen in this book. Another indication is the growing number of companies – developers, investors and service companies – that are crossing frontiers to carry out international business operations. Furthermore, the regulation of certain activities is being transposed from one country to another. One example of this are the real estate investment trusts (REITs), which began in 1960 in the USA and are now present in most of the world's developed countries. They were introduced into the UK, Germany and Italy in 2007.

This growing internationalization is being driven by a number of factors; in particular, the growth of real estate companies and funds, which need geographical diversification in order to meet their growth goals. Another reason is to be found in the management of real estate investment risk. Cross-border operations are also stimulated by the growing transparency of the property markets resulting from the increasing entry of professional operators, the activity of service companies and consultants, the provision of information on returns and indices, and – to some extent – government regulations. While the increasing internationalization is standardizing practices, and to a certain point returns, a low correlation is still seen in investment returns in different countries.

This internationalization process has also been felt in Europe. There are already many companies that operate in more than one country, and practices and procedures are becoming increasingly similar. Institutions from other continents have also contributed to this internationalization, primarily American real estate companies and funds. Because of this, and the strengthening of the idea of a united Europe through the enlargement of the European Union, it is useful to have a broad vision of the European real estate markets as a whole. This vision is so far only available – and not completely – to the international operators mentioned above.

No one will deny that the idea of writing a book about European property markets is challenging. But it is necessary and – one hopes – useful for real estate operators and researchers on the subject. The first decision that must be made is which countries to include in the book, as the frontiers of Europe are not fixed or accepted by everyone. A purely technical issue helps to solve this problem: basically, the availability of information, though wherever we can we have taken the widest possible view of Europe. This has been the case, for example, in dealing with housing and mortgage markets, for which more complete information is available throughout Europe. However, we have had to be much more restrictive when discussing, for example, commercial real estate, where the information available is sometimes limited to the largest cities in the countries that have been long-standing members of the EU.

In many parts of the book, the European Union is cited in the abbreviate form EU followed by a number, indicating the composition of the EU reflected in those data; that is, the number of countries that formed the EU at that time. Table I.1 lists the varying composition of the EU, including the current Euro Zone.

Of course, an important part of this book, even though it does not have the greatest number of pages devoted to it, is the harmonization or integration effort undertaken by EU institutions. Although the role of the European institutions, and that of regulation in particular, is still a subject of debate, steps have been taken in the study and proposal of measures that seek integration – particularly in the financial aspects of real estate markets.

The book covers four subjects: the description of the main markets; the risk and return profile of real estate investment; indirect vehicles of investment – that is, real estate companies and funds; and the financial side of real estate activity. Chapter 1 covers the housing markets and their main determinants, such as population and households. The comparisons between European countries reveal the social and political differences that exist among them, which in turn lead to significant differences in the types of dwellings, tenancy systems and government policies. As it would take up too much space to talk about the housing policies implemented in each country, and as there are similarities among all of them, a few countries have been chosen as being representative of the main public policies on the subject.

Chapter 2 deals with commercial real estate: basically offices, retail, and industrial and logistics properties. The main feature of these products is that they are the most international, both in development, and in investment and finance. They usually make up the major part of international real estate agents' business, which makes them a very important source of information. As a general rule, this type of asset

Table I.1   Composition of the European Union

Countries	Entry year				
Belgium	1950				
France	1950				
Germany	1950				
Netherlands	1950				Euro
Italy	1950				Zone
Luxembourg	1950	EU-12			
Republic of Ireland	1973	(founded			
Greece	1981	in 1993)	EU-15		
Portugal	1986				
Spain	1986				
Denmark	1973				
United Kingdom	1973			EU-25	
Sweden	1995			EU-27	
Austria	1995				
Finland	1995				Euro
Cyprus	2004				Zone
Malta	2004				
Slovenia	2004				
Czech Republic	2004				
Estonia	2004				
Hungary	2004				
Latvia	2004				
Lithuania	2004				
Poland	2004				
Slovakia	2004				
Bulgaria	2007				
Romania	2007				

is more associated with cities, and the volume and quantity of information available varies considerably, depending on the markets' size and maturity. Consequently, it is more difficult to obtain reliable information about the younger markets, leading to significant disparities in the availability of information, and therefore on the possibility of covering a range of cities.

Chapter 3 deals with the results of direct investment in property. Property investment is viewed as one of the 'alternative investments', complementary to financial investment in equities, bonds, and short-term financial assets. However, this type of investment has always been very common, and continues to be the leading non-financial investment. The proportion of property in the portfolios of certain non-real estate institutional investors, such as pension funds, is increasing, and other investors who had announced their intention not to invest in real estate – such as the private equity funds – are now major players in corporate and asset transactions in the real estate industry. Chapter 3 analyses the risk and return obtained in recent years in the various asset classes, and presents a few long-term series that compare the returns on real estate compared with stocks and bonds.

Chapter 4 provides a description of the main operators in the European property markets, basically listed real estate companies and real estate investment funds, and shows the dichotomy among financial analysts between public (listed companies) and private investments (funds). As a result of the greater weight of international transactions, it has become increasingly important for the operators in each European country to be aware of the features of the main companies and funds operating in Europe. It is becoming increasingly common to find an investor or lender from one European country doing business in another country. An insight into their features, including their financial performance, would be useful for all parties. This chapter also includes an Appendix detailing property investment by insurance companies and pension funds, an important group of non-real estate institutions that invest in properties.

The last two chapters discuss the financial markets related to the real estate sector: the mortgage loan market, which is the instrument used by institutions to finance themselves; and the derivatives that have been developed from this. Chapter 5 is concerned with the primary market – the mortgage loans themselves. It describes the different markets, with very complete information for Europe, both at the level of balances outstanding and on lending activity. A classification is provided of the different types of mortgage loans and the institutions that operate in each country. The low volume of the mortgage markets at the time of writing in the countries that have recently become members of the EU, and their current development, lead us to think that the property markets will grow in these countries. One consequence of increasing lending activity is the greater level of household indebtedness in almost all European countries, although the present situation varies widely from one country to another.

Finally, Chapter 6 addresses the secondary mortgage markets used by the financial institutions to obtain funding. It discusses the sources of finance that are linked most closely to real estate activity, focusing mainly on the funding instruments mentioned earlier: the mortgage bonds, the mortgage-backed securities, and the derivatives that have been formed from these. All these funding instruments have had exceptionally high issuance levels in recent years, because of the strong growth in mortgage lending, but this growth has not been accompanied by a similar growth in the most traditional source of funds, deposits. In fact, a large part of the operators on the mortgage markets, who have benefited from the rapid increase in lending, are not normal deposit-taking institutions. The securitization activity has involved a very diverse range of operators (for example, rating agencies and insurance companies) who have also benefited from the increased volume.

Both Chapter 5 and Chapter 6 explain the role of the European Union institutions in the harmonization and integration of the European mortgage markets and the markets that contribute to the financial institutions' funding. Since the summer of 2007, the international financial markets have been affected dramatically by events directly related to or deriving from the real estate markets. They are all part of a sequence, consisting of the deceleration of the favourable housing cycle that most Western countries have experienced; a deterioration in the quality of certain mortgage loans in the banks' assets, starting with the subprime mortgages in the USA; a devaluation of the securities tied to these mortgages; the subsequent financial squeeze; and, most recently, an incipient deterioration in the condition of the commercial real estate market (at least, in offices in some of the more active markets, such as the UK). From the beginning of that process there was a fluent and negative interaction between the financial and the real estate markets. These circumstances have a bearing on almost all of the issues discussed in this book, and consequently are addressed in the different chapters when objective data are available.

Because the USA is a very relevant country in the real estate and financial international arena, comments on the US situation have been included in some parts of the book, normally boxed in order to separate them from the analysis of European issues.

Many people have helped the author in writing this book and it is only fair to acknowledge them. First, the research assistants who have played an active part in collecting and analysing the data and correcting different parts of the book; in particular, Amparo Vassallo, now manager of the CIIF (see below), and Guillermo Bruzon, Natalia Muñoz and Reyes Casanueva. The author would also like to thank the students enrolled on IESE Business School's Real Estate Firm Management course, in the MBA Programme and the Executive Programmes for their illuminating discussion of most parts of this book. The generosity of all the institutions and firms that have provided data used in the book also deserves the author's gratitude. In particular, the author would like to thank Investment Property Databank (IPD) for providing much useful data contributing decisively to Chapter 3. The financial support provided by the IESE's Research Division and its International Centre for Financial Research (CIIF), has been vital for the successful completion of the book. And last, but not least, gratitude goes to the publisher, who has been kind enough to extend the time for writing the book to enable the author to meet his academic obligations.

1
The Residential Sector

In addition to its undoubted social value, housing is also a vitally important component of the general economy. When the people occupying the dwellings are also their owners, the investment usually accounts for a sizeable part of their assets and a determining factor of their financing habits. When the dwelling is rented, payment of the rent represents a significant part of family expenditure.

The dwelling also has a direct impact on other important sectors of the economy. Residential property building accounts for a significant percentage of the construction industry and, consequently, is a prominent source of employment. Housing development activity represents the major part of the development industry. Housing finance stands for a significant amount of the business of financial institutions in many European countries, as will be seen in Chapter 5, and investment in residential property has a significant weight in the investment portfolios of real estate companies. In addition, the 'wealth effect' that determines households' consumption habits depend to a great extent on the value of housing.

The housing markets and the financing of these became a subject of concern for people, financial institutions, house builders and governments in 2007. The most visible aspect of the new situation was the difficulties experienced in the mortgage markets in the USA, at both origination and secondary levels, but also the housing markets themselves showed signs that the existing favourable cycle was turning down. In many countries, both housing activity and house prices are diminishing.

There are more than 224 million dwellings in the EU-27, as we shall see later. One way of highlighting the importance of these is to compare the value of dwellings with other classes of assets. See, for example, Figure 1.1, which shows details for the United Kingdom (UK). The value of the investment in the residential market is more than double the

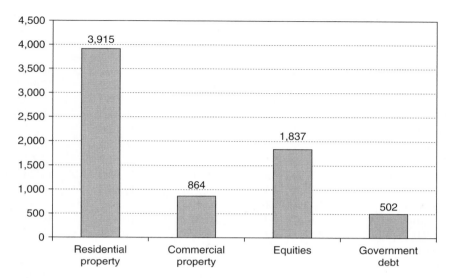

Figure 1.1 Size of UK investment markets, 2006 (in billions of pounds sterling)

Source: Long, M. (2007) 'UK Residential Property Market Overview', presentation at the IPD European Investment Residential Conference.

value of equity capitalization, and several times the value of commercial real estate and government debt.

The basic factors that determine housing demand in a country include, in particular, demographic factors referring to the population and the number of households. For this reason, they will also be the first subject to be discussed in this chapter. This will be followed by a description of the housing stock in the EU and other European countries, annual housing production, and housing transactions. The chapter will end with a brief outline of the various housing policies applied in different European countries.

Population

The countries of the EU-27 had 492.9 million inhabitants (2006), with 79 per cent of the population living in the EU-15, whose population was 389.5 million inhabitants. Among these, Germany had the largest population, with 82.4 million inhabitants, followed by France (62.9 million), the United Kingdom (60.3 million) and Italy (58.7 million). There were eleven countries with fewer than 10 million inhabitants. See Table 1.1.

Table 1.1 Population of Europe (thousands)

	1997	2000	2005	2006
Germany	82,012	82,163	82,501	82,438
France	59,726	60,513	62,519	62,999
UK	58,239	58,785	60,060	60,393
Italy	56,876	56,924	58,462	58,752
Spain	39,525	40,050	43,038	43,758
Poland	38,639	38,654	38,174	38,157
Romania	22,054	21,908	21,659	21,610
Netherlands	15,567	15,864	16,306	16,334
Greece	10,745	10,904	11,083	11,125
Portugal	10,073	10,195	10,529	10,570
Belgium	10,170	10,239	10,446	10,511
Czech Republic	10,309	10,278	10,221	10,251
Hungary	10,301	10,222	10,098	10,077
Sweden	8,844	8,861	9,011	9,048
Austria	7,965	8,002	8,207	8,266
Bulgaria	8,341	8,191	7,761	7,719
Denmark	5,275	5,330	5,411	5,427
Slovakia	5,379	5,399	5,385	5,389
Finland	5,132	5,171	5,237	5,256
Republic of Ireland	3,655	3,778	4,109	4,209
Lithuania	3,588	3,512	3,425	3,403
Latvia	2,445	2,382	2,306	2,295
Slovenia	1,987	1,988	1,998	2,003
Estonia	1,406	1,372	1,348	1,345
Cyprus	666	690	749	766
Luxembourg	417	434	455	460
Malta	374	380	403	404
EU-15	374,223	377,213	387,373	389,545
[EU-27	479,712	482,188	490,898	492,965]
Russia	n.a.	n.a.	143,500	142,800
Turkey	63,485	65,787	71,610	72,521
Ukraine	50,600	49,900	46,930	46,646
Serbia	7,831	7,773	7,441	7,463
Switzerland	7,081	7,124	7,415	7,459
Norway	4,393	4,478	4,606	4,640
Croatia	4,572	4,442	4,444	4,443
Iceland	270	279	294	300

Source: European Mortgage Federation (2007) *Hypostat 2006* (November).

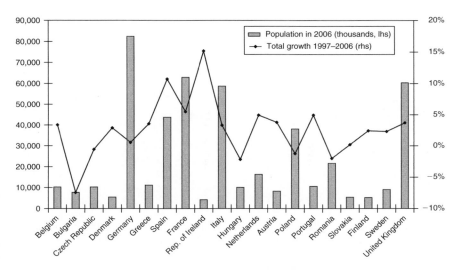

Figure 1.2 Population in Europe, 2006, and total growth, 1997–2006
Source: European Mortgage Federation (2007) *Hypostat 2006* (November).

Outside the EU, the countries with the largest populations were Russia (142.8 million) and Turkey (72.5 million).

Among the EU-27 countries with populations greater than 4 million people, population growth from 1997 to 2006 has been greatest in Ireland and Spain, with 15.2 per cent and 10.7 per cent, respectively; see Figure 1.2. The other countries have grown at rates ranging between −7.5 per cent in Bulgaria and 5.5 per cent in France. In addition to Bulgaria, negative growth rates are also found in Hungary, Poland and Romania.

Taking a longer-term view, we can see that population growth between 1980 and 2006 was greatest in the Netherlands (61.7 per cent), Iceland (36.4 per cent) and Ireland (23.8 per cent); see Figure 1.3. Switzerland, Spain, Greece, Norway and Austria have also grown at double-digit rates. The other countries have also grown, but at a slower rate, and only Hungary experienced negative growth during this period.

Population density

Excluding Malta, which has by far the greatest population density in Europe, and Iceland, for the opposite reason, the mean density of thirty-one European countries is 127.1 inhabitants per square kilometre. The EU-25 has a density of 116 inhabitants/km^2. The Netherlands, Belgium and the United Kingdom are the countries with the greatest population

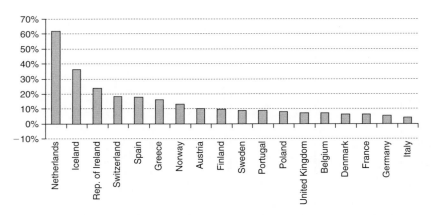

Figure 1.3   Variation in the population of Europe, by country, 1980–2006
Source: European Mortgage Federation (2007) *Hypostat 2006* (November).

densities, with more than 240 inhabitants per km². Table 1.2 lists the European countries for which information is available. The countries with the lowest population density are Sweden, Finland and Norway, with 22, 17.5 and 15.2 inhabitants per km², respectively.

Population projections

According to the United Nations' projections for 2050, while the world population will increase by 37.8 per cent (from 6.671 billion to 9.191 billion inhabitants), Europe will be the only continent whose population will decrease, from 731 million to 664 million inhabitants; that is, 9.2 per cent less; see Table 1.3. This data is based on the scenario predicted by the UN using a medium-variant fertility rate.

The estimated population in the EU-27 countries for 2050 is 479.5 million inhabitants, 2.7 per cent less than in 2006. It is forecast that the greatest increases will take place in Luxembourg and Ireland, with 54.6 per cent and 43.7 per cent increases over the entire period, respectively; see Table 1.4. The population will fall in all of the Central and Eastern European countries. Among the largest countries, the population will fall by 10.3 per cent in Germany, and increase by 10.7 per cent and 13.1 per cent in France and the UK, respectively. Outside the EU, the population will fall most sharply in Ukraine and Russia (by 33.0 per cent and 24.3 per cent, respectively) and increase the most in Turkey (by 32.1 per cent).

Part of the expected variation in Europe comes from migration. Europe had negative migratory balances (more emigrants than immigrants)

Table 1.2 Population density, selected
European countries, 2005–6 (inhabitants
per sq km)

Malta	1278.6
Netherlands	483.1
Belgium	345.5
United Kingdom	247.4
Germany	230.9
Liechtenstein	217.2
Italy	198.6
Switzerland	185.9
Luxembourg	176.8
Czech Republic	132.5
Denmark	125.7
Poland	122.1
France	114.7
Portugal	114.5
Slovakia	109.9
Hungary	108.4
Austria	99.9
Slovenia	99.3
Romania	94.1
Turkey	93.6
Spain	86.8
Greece	84.9
Cyprus	81.9
Croatia	78.5
Bulgaria	69.7
Republic of Ireland	60.8
Lithuania	54.5
Latvia	36.9
Estonia	31.0
Sweden	22.0
Finland	17.2
Norway	15.2
Iceland	3.0

Note: The data for France, Spain and UK have been
estimated for 2006 from *Hypostat 2006*; the remain-
der is for 2005 from Eurostat.
Sources: Eurostat (http://epp.eurostat.ec.europa.eu);
European Mortgage Federation (2007) *Hypostat 2006*
(November).

Table 1.3 Global population forecast for 2050, by continent (millions of people)

	1950	1975	2007	2050
World	2,535	4,076	6,671	9,191
More developed regions	814	1,048	1,223	1,245
Less developed regions	1,722	3,028	5,448	7,946
Least developed countries	201	358	804	1,742
Other less developed countries	1,521	2,670	4,644	6,204
Africa	224	416	965	1,998
Asia	1,411	2,394	4,030	5,266
Europe	548	676	731	664
Latin America and the Caribbean	168	325	572	769
North America	172	243	339	445
Oceania	13	21	34	49

Source: United Nations (2007) *World Population Prospects: The 2006 Revision* (New York: UN).

until the 1970s, but since that time the balance has been positive and growing steadily, until the decade of 2000–10, when it is expected to peak; see Table 1.5. For the period 2011–50, it is expected that the net annual migratory balance will amount to about 800,000 people on average.

The change in the population will be one of the key factors in housing demand. It is expected that the European population will age during this period, until 2050. This factor will increase the demand for housing for senior citizens. By 2050, Europe will have the highest proportion of people aged over 65, who will account for 27.6 per cent of its population; see Figure 1.4. This is followed by North America, with more than 20 per cent, while in Oceania, Latin America and the Caribbean, the percentage of people aged over 65 will range between 15 per cent and 20 per cent. The lowest proportion of the population aged over 65 is expected to be in Africa, with 6.7 per cent.

The population is expected to age in all of the EU-27 countries. By 2050, the country with the smallest population aged over 60 (Luxembourg, with 31.8 per cent) will have a larger elderly population than the country with the largest elderly population in 2005 (Italy, with 30.4 per cent); see Figure 1.5. Italy, Germany and Greece are among the five countries with the greatest population aged over 60 in both 2005 and in 2050. Ireland and Cyprus are two countries among the five countries with the lowest elderly population in both 2005 and 2050.

Table 1.4 Population forecast for 2050, Europe, by country (millions and percentage variation)

	2050	Growth 2006–50 (%)
Austria	8,500	1.7
Belgium	10,643	1.8
Bulgaria	4,949	−35.2
Cyprus	1,183	38.4
Czech Republic	8,825	−13.4
Denmark	5,528	1.6
Estonia	1,128	−15.5
Finland	5,360	1.6
France	68,270	10.7
Germany	74,088	−10.3
Greece	10,808	−3.0
Hungary	8,459	−15.7
Republic of Ireland	6,179	43.7
Italy	54,610	−7.2
Latvia	1,768	−22.4
Lithuania	2,654	−21.7
Luxembourg	722	54.6
Malta	428	5.2
Netherlands	17,235	5.0
Poland	30,260	−20.5
Portugal	9,982	−6.0
Romania	15,928	−25.7
Slovakia	4,664	−13.5
Slovenia	1,694	−15.4
Spain	46,401	4.8
Sweden	10,481	14.9
UK	68,717	13.1
Iceland	355	17.9
Norway	5,732	22.0
Russia	107,832	−24.3
Serbia	9,635	−2.3
Switzerland	8,434	12.7
Turkey	98,946	32.1
Ukraine	30,937	−33.0

Source: United Nations (2007) *World Population Prospects: The 2006 Revision* (New York: UN).

Table 1.5 Average net annual number of international migrants, by decade, 1950–2050 (thousands)

	1951–60	1961–70	1971–80	1981–90	1991–2000	2001–10	2011–20	2021–30	2030–2040	2040–2050
Africa	−125	−242	−289	−267	−310	−416	−377	−395	−393	−393
Asia	194	−22	−377	−451	−1340	−1311	−1210	−1221	−1222	−1222
Europe	−489	−31	288	444	1051	1271	799	805	808	808
Latin America and the Caribbean	−68	−293	−415	−781	−775	−1108	−616	−590	−595	−595
North America	403	479	748	972	1277	1453	1305	1300	1300	1300
Oceania	85	109	44	86	96	111	99	101	102	102

Source: United Nations (2007) *World Population Prospects: The 2006 Revision* (New York: UN).

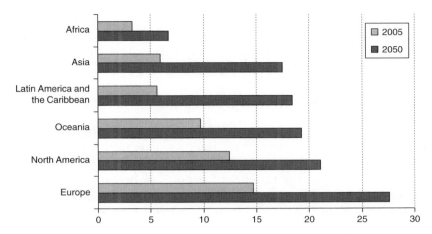

Figure 1.4 Ageing of the global population, 2005 and 2050, by continent (percentage of people aged over 65)
Source: Ministry of Employment of Spain (2006) *Elderly People in Spain: Report.*

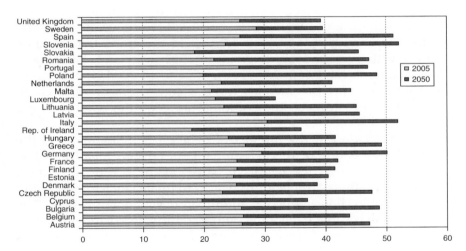

Figure 1.5 Ageing of the population in EU-27 countries, 2005 and 2050 (percentage of people aged over 60)
Source: United Nations (2007) *World Population Prospects: The 2006 Revision* (New York: UN).

The United Kingdom moves down from ninth place in terms of population aged over 60 in 2005 to twenty-third place in 2050.

Other European countries will also have an ageing population. For example, in Ukraine and Croatia, where the percentage of the population aged over 60 will increase from 23.2 per cent and 25 per cent, respectively, in 2005, to 43.7 per cent and 44.5 per cent, respectively, in 2050. In Russia, the elderly population is estimated to grow from 19.2 per cent to 38.2 per cent of the total population.

Characteristics of European households

The households also determine the size and characteristics of the long-term housing demand, including sizes of dwellings and number of bedrooms.

There is a trend for the number of people per household to decrease in most countries. The countries where the size of the households has fallen most are those that had larger households in the 1990s – with more than three people per household: Spain, Ireland and Portugal; see Table 1.6. The largest decrease has been observed in Spain. Sociological changes, such as the fall in the birth rate, longer life expectancy, an increase in single-person households, among other factors, will determine the features of future dwellings.

At a more detailed level, a change is seen in the number of members that comprise the family from the 1980s to the time of writing (2008). There has been a marked decrease in the proportion of larger families, which was the largest group in 1981 in Ireland, Poland and some Mediterranean countries; see Figure 1.6. In 2004, the group of households with just one member was the largest in most of the countries studied, in particular the Scandinavian countries, Germany and the UK.

The combination of the number of people per household and the dwelling's size is one of the determinants of citizens' quality of life. The size of dwellings reflects need, based on the size of the family, together with other considerations related to financial factors and individual countries' housing policy and urban development history. The size of dwellings varies depending on the country. In Poland, for example, the most common size of dwelling (of 35.6 per cent of families) is less than $50\,\text{m}^2$; see Table 1.7. Dwellings of between 50 and $74\,\text{m}^2$ are mainly found in Ireland (65.5 per cent), Hungary (36.3 per cent), Germany (31.5 per cent), and Finland (29.8 per cent). Dwellings with areas of between 75 and $99\,\text{m}^2$ are most common in Greece (29.7 per cent) and France (26.5 per cent). Finally, those measuring $100–149\,\text{m}^2$ are most common in Denmark (31 per cent), Norway (30.8 per cent), Italy (29.5 per cent) and Austria (27.3 per cent).

Families' spending on housing accounts for 21 per cent of their total spending in the EU-25. The Scandinavian countries allocate a higher

Table 1.6 Size of European households, 1993 and 2003 (average number of people per household)

	1993	2003	Difference 1993–2003
EU-25 countries	n.a.	2.4	
EU-15 countries	n.a.	2.4	
Euro area (12 countries)	n.a.	2.4	
Belgium	2.5	2.5	0.0
Bulgaria	n.a.	2.7	
Czech Republic	n.a.	2.5	
Denmark	n.a.	2.2	
Germany	2.3	2.1	−0.2
Estonia	n.a.	2.6	
Republic of Ireland	3.2	2.9	−0.3
Greece	2.8	2.6	−0.2
Spain	3.3	2.9	−0.4
France	2.5	2.4	−0.1
Italy	2.8	2.6	−0.2
Cyprus	n.a.	3.0	
Latvia	n.a.	2.8	
Lithuania	n.a.	2.9	
Luxembourg	2.7	2.5	−0.2
Hungary	n.a.	2.6	
Malta	n.a.	3.0	
Netherlands	2.4	2.3	−0.1
Austria	n.a.	2.4	
Poland	n.a.	3.1	
Portugal	3.1	2.8	−0.3
Romania	n.a.	2.8	
Slovenia	n.a.	2.6	
Slovakia	n.a.	3.1	
Finland	n.a.	2.2	
United Kingdom	2.4	2.3	−0.1

Source: Eurostat (accessed June 2008).

proportion of their spending to housing (about 29 per cent), compared with the United Kingdom, Greece or Spain, where spending on housing is 17 per cent; see Figure 1.7. The variation in household spending on housing is related to the evolution of house prices. Thus, between the years 2000 and 2005, the largest increase in housing spending was in Spain (almost 3 points) and the Netherlands (2.5 points). On the other

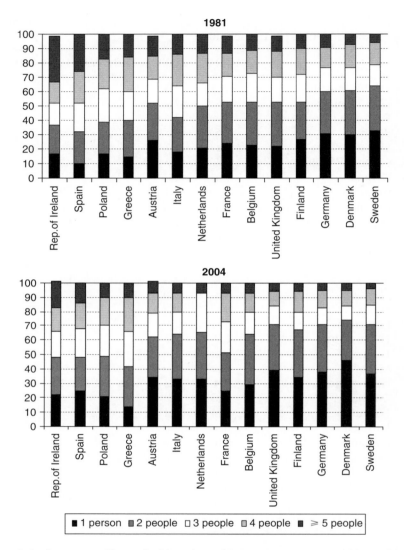

Figure 1.6   Structure of households, selected European countries, 1981 and 2004 (composition of households based on number of members)

Source: Ministry of Infrastructure of the Italian Republic (2006) *Housing Statistics in the European Union. 2005/2006* (Federcasa, Italian Housing Federation, September).

hand, such spending fell by 2 points in Poland. One variable related to family expenditure on housing is the level of borrowing by those who have decided to buy the dwelling in which they live; this is discussed in Chapter 5.

Table 1.7 Size of dwellings, selected European countries, various years (number of dwellings and percentage of dwellings of each size)

	Austria 2004	Denmark 2002	Finland 2004	France 2002	Germany 2002	Poland 2002	Greece 2001	Hungary 2005	Rep. of Ireland 2002	Italy 1991	Norway 2001
Total dwellings (1000s)	3,429	2,409	2,402	24,525	35,033	13,331	3,548	3,997	1,387	19,909	1,962
under 50 m² (%)	11.9	6.1	22	13.6	11.2	35.6	10.1	14.9	12.9	7.9	8.5
50 m² to 74 m² (%)	24.8	20.8	29.8	25.6	31.5	33.1	28.9	36.3	65.5	52.7	21.9
75 m² to 99 m² (%)	23.1	23.4	21.0	26.5	22.6	12.0	29.7	23.0	n.a.	n.a.	15.8
100 m² to 149 m² (%)	27.3	31.0	20.9	24.9	25.7	13.2	26.3	21.4	21.6	29.5	30.8
150 m² and more (%)	12.9	18.5	5.3	9.5	9.1	6.0	5.1	4.4	n.a.	9.0	23.0

Source: United Nations Economic Commission for Europe (2006) *Bulletin of Housing Statistics for Europe and North America.*

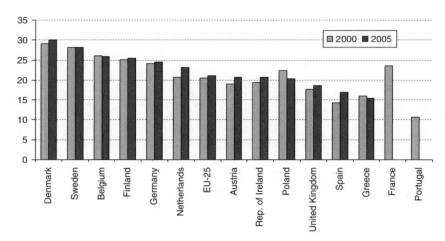

Figure 1.7   Family spending on housing, EU-25 and selected European countries, 2000 and 2005 (percentage of total expenditure)
Note: The data for Sweden, Belgium, Finland, Spain, France, Portugal and EU-25 correspond to 2004.
Source: Ministry of Infrastructure of the Italian Republic (2006) *Housing Statistics in the European Union. 2005/2006* (Federcasa, Italian Housing Federation, September).

Housing stock

Without considering Malta, there are 224.1 million dwellings in the EU-27; see Table 1.8. The countries with the most dwellings are also those with the most population: Germany, France, Italy, the UK and Spain, which together account for 53.4 per cent of all dwellings. Excluding Malta, the country with the lowest number of dwellings is Luxembourg, with 125,200 units. Estonia and Slovenia also have fewer than a million houses each. Outside the EU, Turkey and Ukraine stand out as having the greatest number of houses.

Table 1.8 also shows the growth in the number of dwellings between 1997 and 2006. Of the countries with data for this period, the growth of Ireland (58 per cent), Spain (29 per cent), and Cyprus (27 per cent) stand out. These are countries that have experienced a boom in housing development. Portugal, with a 16 per cent growth in the number of houses during the period, and Poland, with a 12 per cent growth, are also remarkable.

The ages of dwellings reflects the reconstruction of the housing stock after the Second World War, which severely reduced the housing stock in many European countries. The largest number of properties in Europe were built between 1946 and 1980; see Figure 1.8. The age of the

Table 1.8 Total housing stock, Europe, 1997 and 2006 (thousands of units)

	1997	2006	Variation 1997–2006 (%)
Germany	37,050	39,740	7
France	28,267	29,133	3
Italy	26,406	26,548	1
UK	24,721	26,194	6
Spain	19,122	24,678	29
Poland	11,613	12,987	12
Romania	7,837	8,231	5
Netherlands	6,441	6,912	7
Portugal	4,760	5,520	16
Greece	5,116	5,329	4
Belgium	n.a.	4,903	
Czech Republic	n.a.	4,516	
Sweden	4,260	4,436	4
Hungary	4,005	4,238	6
Bulgaria	n.a.	3,729	
Austria	3,610	3,727	3
Finland	2,416	2,669	10
Denmark	2,479	2,645	7
Slovakia	n.a.	1,955	
Republic of Ireland	1,144	1,805	5
Lithuania	1,278	1,307	2
Latvia	n.a.	1,004	
Slovenia	690	805	17
Estonia	620	638	3
Cyprus	268	341	27
Luxembourg	114	125	10
EU-27 without Malta		224,115	
Ukraine	18,784	19,132	2
Turkey	n.a.	16,236	
Switzerland	3,472	3,792	9
Serbia	n.a.	3,023	
Norway	1,885	2,055	9
Iceland	n.a.	120	

Note: The latest data for Finland, Luxembourg, Slovenia, UK, Iceland, Norway and Ukraine are from 2005. The latest data for Austria, France, Greece and Turkey are from the year 2000.
Source: European Mortgage Federation (2007) *Hypostat 2006* (November).

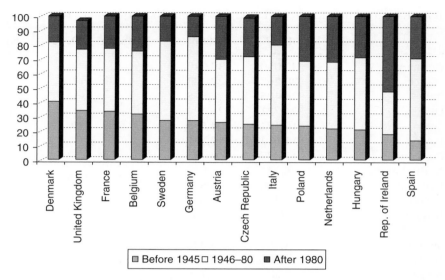

Figure 1.8 Age of the housing stock, selected European countries, 2005–6 (percentage of housing stock by age group)

Note: Data for Belgium, France, Italy, Poland, Spain and the United Kingdom include only houses built before the year 2000.

Source: Ministry of Infrastructure of the Italian Republic (2006) *Housing Statistics in the European Union, 2005/2006* (Federcasa, Italian Housing Federation, September).

properties in certain countries, such as Denmark, the United Kingdom or France is worth noting, as more than a third of these countries' housing stock was built before 1945. The opposite is the case in the Republic of Ireland, where approximately 20 per cent of its dwellings have been built since the 1980s.

The mean number of dwellings in the EU-27 countries is 457.5 per 1,000 inhabitants (this calculation does not include Malta, for which no data have been obtained); see Figure 1.9. Spain is the country with the most dwellings per inhabitant, with 564 dwellings per 1.000 of the population. The country that comes closest to the EU-27 average is Italy. Luxembourg, Poland, Hungary, the Netherlands, the Republic of Ireland and the United Kingdom are all below the average. As is to be expected, some of these countries have the largest number of people per household – for example, the Republic of Ireland and Hungary, with 2.9 and 2.5 people per household, respectively.

Outside the EU, Iceland, Serbia and Ukraine have between 400 and 410 dwellings per 1,000 inhabitants, Norway has 442 and Switzerland has 552.

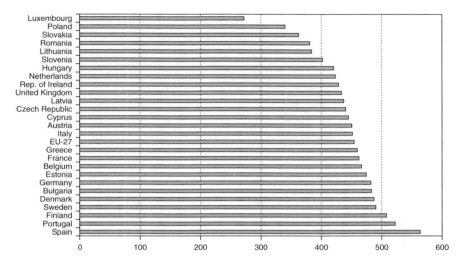

Figure 1.9   Housing stock in relation to the population, EU-27 countries, 2006 (number of dwellings per 1,000 inhabitants)
Note: The data for Finland, Luxembourg, Slovenia, the United Kingdom, Republic of Ireland, Norway and Ukraine are from 2005. The data for Austria, France, Greece and Italy are from the year 2000.
Source: European Mortgage Federation *Hypostat 2006* (November 2007).

Housing density varies considerably across Europe: see Figure 1.10, which shows the density in the seventeen countries that have available data. The countries with the highest housing density have 100–200 dwellings per km^2; these are the Netherlands, Belgium, Germany and the United Kingdom, which are also the four countries with the highest population density (not including Malta). At the next level there are the countries with a mean density of between 40 and 90 dwellings per km^2: Italy, Denmark, Portugal, France, Austria, Spain, Luxembourg, Hungary, Poland and Greece. Finally, there are the countries with fewer than 30 dwellings per km^2, and which have low population densities (see Table 1.2), namely, the Republic of Ireland, Sweden and Finland.

Unoccupied dwellings

Italy is the country with the largest percentage of unoccupied dwellings, with 19.6 per cent of the total stock in 2001; see Figure 1.11 the countries with available data. Italy is followed by Spain, with 13.9 per cent for the same year; and Ireland with 10.1 per cent. This figure for unoccupied dwellings is significant for Spain and Ireland as they are countries with a high housing construction rate and high growth in house prices in

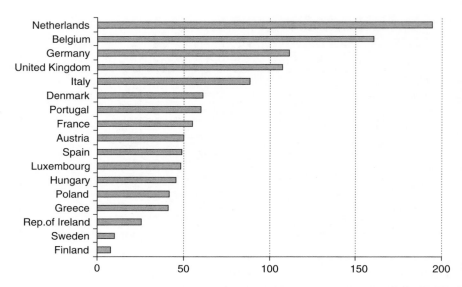

Figure 1.10 Housing density, selected European countries, 2006 (dwellings per km^2)

Source: European Mortgage Federation (2007) *Hypostat 2006* (November).

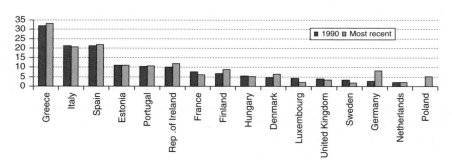

Figure 1.11 Unoccupied dwellings, selected European countries, 1990 and most recent (unoccupied dwellings as percentage of total stock)

Note: The most recent data for Italy, Spain, Portugal, Greece and Luxembourg are from 2001. The data for Hungary, Denmark and Sweden are from 2005 and the rest from 2002. Second homes should be excluded, but in practice some countries may include them. This may help to explain some high values, but also make comparisons more difficult.

Source: Ministry of Infrastructure of the Italian Republic (2006) *Housing Statistics in the European Union, 2005/2006* (Federcasa, Italian Housing Federation, September).

recent years. At the other extreme, the three countries with the lowest percentage of unoccupied dwellings are Luxembourg (2.4 per cent), Netherlands (2.2 per cent) and Sweden (1.7 per cent).

Forms of occupancy: ownership and rental

Within the EU-27, the highest proportions of owner-occupied houses are to be found in Romania, Lithuania, Bulgaria and Hungary – all greater than 90 per cent. (The remaining households in each of these countries live in rented houses, and some of the countries have a small proportion of occupancy other than by direct ownership or rental, such as houses owned by occupiers' co-operatives.) Rates for owner-occupied houses of between 80 per cent and 90 per cent are found in Estonia, Spain, Latvia and Slovenia. The countries with the lowest proportions of owner-occupiers are Germany (43.2 per cent) and the Czech Republic (47 per cent), while France, the Netherlands, Austria, Finland and Sweden each have 50–58 per cent of owner-occupiers. The average rate for the EU-27 is 67 per cent. Outside the EU, the country with the highest proportion of owner-occupied houses is Croatia (96.1 per cent) and the country with the lowest proportion is Switzerland (34.6 per cent). See Table 1.9.

The forms of occupancy, basically ownership and rental, are both the target and the consequence of government housing policies. Some of the trends in these policies will be discussed later in this chapter.

Housing production

The production of new houses can be measured using three variables: building permits; housing starts; and housing completions over certain periods of time. Building permits tend to match housing starts, particularly during housing booms, as it would be prudent to start as many houses as possible. The same thing happens with housing starts and housing completions, which also match with a couple of years' offset during the favourable part of the housing cycle (the time between the date when house-building begins and its completion, which may be more than two years in the case of dwellings that form part of a block but less for detached houses).

Building permits

The high number of building permits issued in Spain is striking: 865,561 in 2006, which is 54 per cent more than France and three times the number issued in Germany; see Table 1.10. Spain already had the most building permits in 1997, which is when the housing development cycle

Table 1.9 Percentage of owner-occupied houses, Europe, various years

	Latest data available	**Owner-occupation rate (%)**
Romania	2002	97.2
Lithuania	2005	97.0
Bulgaria	2002	96.5
Hungary	2003	92.0
Latvia	2006	87.0
Spain	2005	86.3
Estonia	2002	85.0
Slovenia	2003	84.0
Italy	2002	80.0
Slovakia	2006	79.0
Portugal	2006	76.0
Greece	2006	75.0
Poland	2004	75.0
Luxembourg	2005	74.6
Republic of Ireland	2006	74.5
Malta	2005	74.1
United Kingdom	2005	70.0
Cyprus	2001	68.3
Belgium	2001	68.0
Finland	2005	58.0
Austria	2003	57.0
France	2004	56.5
Denmark	2006	55.0
Netherlands	2002	54.2
Sweden	2005	50.0
Czech Republic	2001	47.0
Germany	2002	43.2
EU-27	/	67.0
Croatia	2006	96.1
Serbia	2002	89.0
Iceland	2006	80–82
Norway	2001	77.0
Turkey	2000	68.3
Russia	2003	63.8
Switzerland	2000	34.6
Ukraine	n.a.	n.a.

Source: European Mortgage Federation (2007) *Hypostat 2006* (November).

Table 1.10   Building permits for housing units, Europe, 1997 and 2006

	1997	2006	Variation 1997–2006 (%)
EU countries			
Spain	337,730	865,561	156.3
France	299,400	561,700	87.6
Germany	530,263	247,541	−53.3
Poland	62,000	160,545	158.9
Netherlands	101,501	96,447	−5.0
Greece	69,867	81,301	16.4
Portugal	44,200	68,615	55.2
Austria	56,925	n.a.	
Belgium	50,194	60,962	21.5
Romania	n.a.	51,065	
Czech Republic	30,819	49,777	61.5
Hungary	n.a.	44,826	
Italy	34,910	n.a.	
Finland	32,750	35,465	8.3
Republic of Ireland	13,729	n.a.	
Sweden	12,500	30,500	144.0
Denmark	17,947	29,180	62.6
Slovakia	12,844	20,592	60.3
Estonia	1,334	12,852	863.4
Malta	3,411	10,409	205.2
Cyprus	6,614	9,794	48.1
Lithuania	n.a.	7,482	
Latvia	n.a.	7,246	
Slovenia	n.a.	6,676	
Luxembourg	3,411	4,411	29.3
Other countries			
Turkey	n.a.	108,109	
Switzerland	33,284	35,416	6.4
Croatia	n.a.	13,575	

Source: European Mortgage Federation (2007) *Hypostat 2006* (November).

can be said to have begun, followed by about ten years of intense housing construction. Excluding the UK and Italy, for which data are not available, Spain, France and Germany are followed by Poland, with 160,545 building permits, and Turkey with 108,109 permits, which is a sign of the growth of housing development in Central and Eastern Europe. Countries such as the Netherlands, Portugal, Belgium,

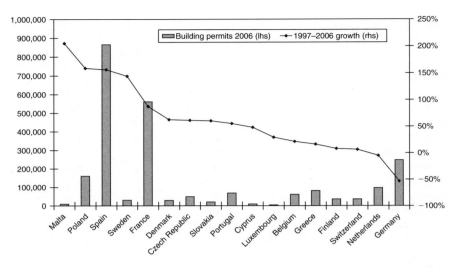

Figure 1.12   Growth in number of building permits, selected European countries, 1997–2006
Source: European Mortgage Federation (2007) *Hypostat 2006* (November).

Hungary, Finland, Sweden, Denmark, Switzerland and Luxembourg, among others, have issued fewer than 100,000 permits.

The housing cycle since the mid-1990s has been favourable for housing development in several countries. Figure 1.12 shows the European countries with data on building permits for 1997 and 2006. Estonia, with a growth of 863.4 per cent during this period, has not been included. There are ten countries that had growth rates above 50 per cent between 1997 and 2006. The behaviour of the countries with the highest volume of permits is striking: Spain and France have grown by156.3 per cent and 87.6 per cent, respectively, while Germany has fallen 53.3 per cent over the same period.

Housing starts

Spain also heads the list for the construction of new housing, with 769,169 new dwellings completed in 2006. This is more than the total produced by the next two countries, France and Italy, and more than three times the housing production in the United Kingdom; see Figure 1.13. Housing starts in the four countries with the greatest building activity (Spain, France, Italy and Germany) were 1,760,070 units in

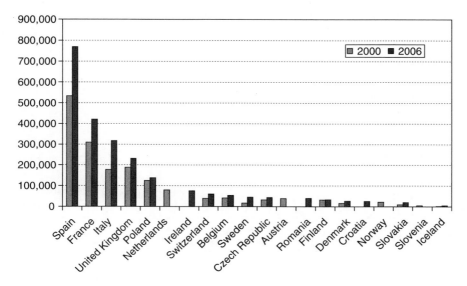

Figure 1.13 Housing starts, selected countries, 2000 and/or 2006
Note: The 2006 data for Romania corresponds to 2005.
Source: European Mortgage Federation (2007) *Hypostat 2006* (November).

2006, while the average figure for housing starts in that year among the countries selected was 196,894. Spain produced almost four times this average, France more than twice, and Italy 1.5 times.

As regards the variations during the period 2000–06, the largest increases are found in Iceland (202 per cent), Sweden (165.7 per cent) (where output rose from 16,900 houses in the year 2000 to 44,900 in 2006), Slovakia (108.3 per cent), and Italy, where output has grown by 78.7 per cent over these years. All the countries in the Figure, apart from Finland, have two-digit growth rates.

It is possible to get an idea of the relative importance of housing production by relating housing starts to the population; see Figure 1.14. The level of activity is particularly high in the Republic of Ireland, Spain and Iceland, with between 17 and 18 housing starts per 1,000 inhabitants. Switzerland, France, Norway, Finland and Croatia show an intermediate level of activity, with between 6 and 8 housing starts per 1,000 inhabitants.

In 2006, many European countries underwent a contraction in housing demand, which was even more intensive in several countries during 2007. Apart from the forecast of an economic downturn, the change

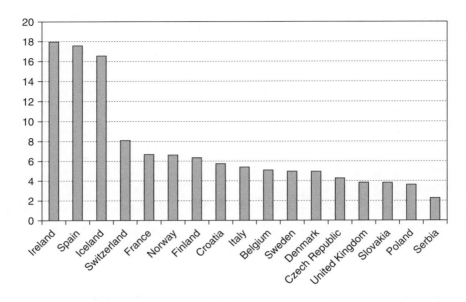

Figure 1.14   Housing starts and population, selected European countries, 2006*
(housing starts per 1,000 inhabitants)
Note: *The data on housing starts for Norway and Serbia correspond to 2005.
Source: European Mortgage Federation (2007) *Hypostat 2006* (November).

was also determined by turbulence in the financial markets, triggered by an increase in the default rate of subprime mortgages (loans granted to people with substandard credit records) in the USA. The result was a financial squeeze that affected many areas, in particular the real estate markets.

This new situation has caused a sharp fall in the housing supply. Housing starts in 2007 were below the level in 2006 in most countries (see Table 1.11); the decrease was 40 per cent in Denmark and over 20 per cent in Spain, Sweden and Croatia.

Housing completions

Spain again heads the list, with 584,881 housing completions in 2006. See Table 1.12. The mean housing completions in all the European countries with data in 2006 is 73,271. After 2000, house production has fallen off in Germany and Portugal with decreases ranging between 27.6 per cent and 45.9 per cent. Outside the EU, house completions dropped in the last decade in Ukraine, Turkey and Croatia.

Table 1.11 Housing starts, selected European countries, 2006 and 2007 (units)

Country	Comparable term	2006	2007	Change (%)
Denmark	Jan–Sep	12,895	7,765	−40
Spain	Jan–Nov	810,000	618,000	−24
Sweden	Jan–Sep	25,900	20,100	−22
Croatia	Jan–Sep	4,981	3,961	−20
Portugal	Jan–Sep	22,620	19,327	−15
Belgium	Jan–Aug	37,129	32,318	−13
Netherlands	Jan–Nov	86,578	76,835	−11
Switzerland	Jan–Sep	19,625	18,917	−4
Norway	full year	32,743	32,287	−1
France	full year	433,940	435,365	0
Finland	Jan–Sep	27,381	30,114	10
Poland	full year	115,353	133,826	16

Source: Thomson DataStream (accessed June 2008).

House transactions and prices

House transactions

The total number of house transactions (understood to mean house purchases or sales) in the thirteen EU-27 countries that present data on this topic amounted to 5.8 million in 2006, 11.4 per cent more than in 2001. The United Kingdom accounted for 30 per cent of these transactions, and it was the country with the largest number of property transactions – a total of 1,777,209 in 2006; see Figure 1.15. The United Kingdom was followed by Spain, with 955,187 transactions, then France and Italy, with about 800,000 transactions each. Germany had 460,000 transactions, and the other selected European countries each had fewer than 250,000 transactions.

The Republic of Ireland, which already had high figures for the number of dwellings being built, building permits and price increases, stands out again, with a 66 per cent increase in property transactions, up from 69,062 in 2001 to 114,593 in 2006. The number of house transactions also increased in Estonia, Italy, United Kingdom, Sweden and Spain, with rates between 12 per cent and 46 per cent. However, falls were observed in the number of transactions in some countries: in decreasing order, these were in the Netherlands, Germany, Finland and Hungary.

Table 1.12   Housing completions, selected European countries (countries with information available for the years indicated)

	1997	2000	2005	2006
EU countries				
Spain	272,333	366,775	524,479	584,881
Germany	570,596	423,062	238,977	248,435
UK	191,075	178,433	209,560	n.a.
Poland	74,000	87,800	114,060	115,187
Republic of Ireland	38,842	49,812	80,957	93,419
Netherlands	92,315	70,650	67,016	72,382
Portugal	78,403	107,887	59,412	58,376
Austria	58,029	53,760	n.a.	n.a.
Belgium	n.a.	40,253	n.a.	n.a.
Romania	n.a.	26,400	32,868	39,638
Hungary	n.a.	21,583	41,084	33,864
Finland	26,854	32,740	34,177	33,683
Sweden	13,000	13,000	23,400	30,300
Czech Republic	16,757	25,207	32,863	30,190
Denmark	17,725	16,414	27,580	25,372
Cyprus	7,148	5,083	16,416	n.a.
Slovakia	7,172	12,931	14,863	14,444
Bulgaria	n.a.	n.a.	12,059	13,270
Slovenia	6,615	6,751	6,272	n.a.
Lithuania	5,562	4,463	5,900	7,286
Luxembourg	2,277	1,671	n.a.	n.a.
Latvia	1,480	899	3,807	5,862
Estonia	1,003	720	3,865	5,082
Other countries				
Ukraine	219,000	63,000	76,000	82,000
Turkey	n.a.	90,849	64,126	65,800
Switzerland	35,961	32,214	37,958	41,989
Norway	18,659	18,873	28,853	n.a.
Serbia	n.a.	10,372	19,500	n.a.
Croatia	12,854	n.a.	4,600	7,200
Iceland	1,369	1,258	3,100	3,294

Source: European Mortgage Federation (2007) *Hypostat 2006* (November).

House prices

According to the data available for house price variations in Europe, the general trend was for prices to increase in 2006. In fact, the only country where prices fell was Germany, by −0.9 per cent; see Table 1.13.

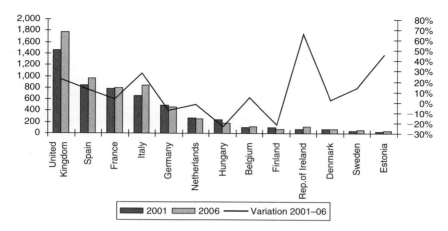

Figure 1.15 Housing transactions, selected EU-27 countries, 2001 and 2006 (000s (lhs) and variations (rhs))
Note: The earliest data available for Germany correspond to 2004. The latest data available for the Netherlands are for 2005, and for the Republic of Ireland, for 2003.
Source: European Mortgage Federation (2007) *Hypostat 2006* (November).

Other price variations in 2006 ranged between 2.1 per cent in Malta to 20.9 per cent in Estonia. The period 1997–2006 was a decade of strong price growth in most of Europe; the countries where prices rose the most were the Republic of Ireland (268.1 per cent), the UK (194.5 per cent), and Spain (168.9 per cent). Price growth in other European countries during 1997–2006 was above 100 per cent, apart from Portugal (48.2 per cent), Switzerland (11.7 per cent), and Germany (−5.7 per cent).

For the countries with data available during the period 1997–2006, the price growth rate has been most volatile in Spain, the Netherlands, Sweden and France. In Germany and the Republic of Ireland, the rates of variation have remained stable, with a slight downward tendency; see Figure 1.16. The greatest oscillations in the rates of price variation are to be found in Spain, with price increases from 2.8 per cent in 1997 to 17.6 per cent in 200, and then falling more than 7 percentage points in 2006.

As with Spain, housing prices in France increased considerably between 1997 and 2003, with the rate of increase going from 2 per cent to 11.5 per cent and then moderating by 1.6 percentage points in 2006. Therefore, the curve plotted for the two countries is similar, though the price variations have been more extreme in the case of Spain. The

Table 1.13   House price variation, selected European countries (annual variation 2006; cumulative variation 1997–2006*)

	2006 (%)	Variation 1997–2006 (%)
Republic of Ireland	13.6	268.1
UK	6.3	184.5
Spain	10.4	168.9
Greece	9.0	167.6
Denmark	16.2	158.7
Netherlands	4.7	145.0
France	9.9	137.1
Sweden	11.4	130.6
Malta	3.5	125.3
Belgium	12.1	121.1
Finland	7.5	106.6
Portugal	2.1	48.2
Germany	−0.9	−5.7
Bulgaria	14.7	
Estonia	20.9	
Austria	3.1	
Slovenia	15.0	
Norway	8.3	111.9
Switzerland	3.3	11.7

Note: *The latest data available for Norway is for 2005, and the cumulative variation is for 1997–2005.
Source: European Mortgage Federation (2007) *Hypostat 2006* (November).

Netherlands and Sweden started the period with rises in the price growth rate (1997–2000), which then moderated in the following period (2000–03), pulling back more sharply in the case of the Netherlands, from 16.5 per cent to 5 per cent. In the final period, the growth rates recovered for both countries, though with greater strength in Sweden, with a 5-percentage-point increase.

The price growth observed up to 2006 is one of the most spectacular in the history of housing prices, for three reasons: its intensity (the rates of price growth); its duration (in some countries, the favourable cycle lasted up to ten years, as in the case of Spain); and the fact that prices have risen simultaneously in many countries. The concurrence of price growth observed in the various countries has been the greatest since the 1970s; see Figure 1.17.

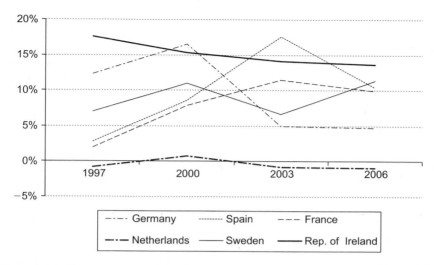

Figure 1.16 House prices, selected European countries, 1997–2006 (percentage annual variation)
Source: European Mortgage Federation (2007) *Hypostat 2006* (November).

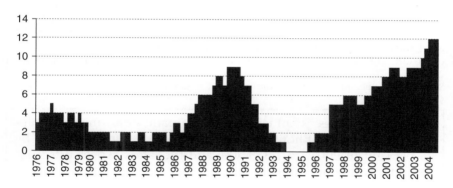

Figure 1.17 Concurrence of favourable cycles in house prices, 1976–2004 (no. of countries with price growth in each year)
Source: OECD (2005): 197.

There are clear signs that the rate of price growth fell in 2007. Although data for the entire year are not yet available, Table 1.14 shows that the rate of price variation fell in all European countries. The largest decreases in price growth rates in Central and Eastern Europe occurred in Lithuania and Latvia; and in Western Europe, in Denmark and the Republic of Ireland, where it has become negative – that is, prices have fallen.

Table 1.14   House prices, selected European countries, annual variation, 2006 and 2007

	End 2006 (%)	2007 (latest) (%)	Reduction of price growth rate (%)
Latvia	69.0	10.2	−58.8
Lithuania	31.0	13.6	−17.3
Republic of Ireland (monthly)	11.8	−4.7	−16.5
Denmark	14.9	4.0	−11.0
Greece	10.5	4.2	−6.4
Estonia (Tallinn)	28.6	23.4	−5.3
Norway	16.7	11.6	−5.1
Spain	9.1	5.3	−3.8
France (Paris)	9.7	8.3	−1.4
Poland	9.7	8.4	−1.3
Germany	3.1	2.0	−1.0
Netherlands	4.7	3.8	−1.0
United Kingdom	10.5	9.7	−0.8
Italy	6.3	5.6	−0.7
Finland	6.6	5.9	−0.7
Switzerland	3.2	2.6	−0.7
Sweden	10.5	9.9	−0.6
Portugal	0.7	0.5	−0.2

Note: The price variation in 2006 differs slightly from that shown in Table 1.12 because of the different sources. However, it is significant that price growth is consistently less in 2007 for all European countries.
Source: www.globalpropertyguide.com (accessed 11 January 2008).

The United States is undergoing a dramatic adjustment of supply. From 1,800,900 housing starts in 2006, the figure dropped by 25 per cent in 2007, to 1,353,900, and the fall is expected to continue during 2008; see Figure 1.18.

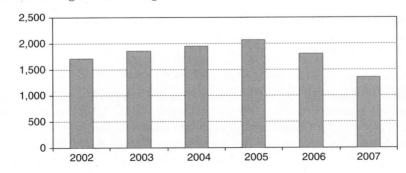

Figure 1.18   Housing starts, USA, 2002–7 (000s of units)

The decrease in supply was caused by the contraction in demand, in addition to other factors that will be addressed later in the book. An estimated 774,000 new residential homes were sold in 2007, which is 26.4 per cent below the 2006 figure of 1,051,000.

In addition to the volume adjustment, the US property business is also immersed in a price-driven adjustment. The year-on-year variation has been falling since the last quarter of 2005, down to a year-on-year variation of 0.4 per cent for the third quarter of 2007. Future year-on-year variations are expected to be negative. The quarterly price variations during 2007 were below 1 per cent, with the third quarter of 2007 being negative: −0.36 per cent; see Figure 1.19.

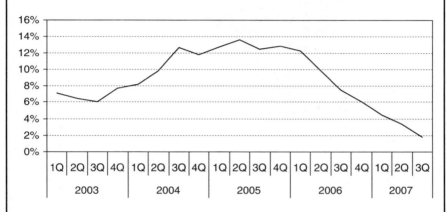

Figure 1.19　OFHEO House Price Index, 2003–7 (year-on-year variation)
Source: Office of Federal Housing Enterprise Oversight House Price Index (OFHEO HPI).

Transaction costs

The transaction costs when buying or selling a house may include taxes, agent's fees, legal fees and registration costs. Belgium is the country with the highest transaction costs, amounting to 17.8 per cent of the price of the property sold, followed by Italy (17 per cent) and France (16.3 per cent); see Figure 1.20. Unlike Belgium and Italy, where sales and transfer taxes on property have a significant weight, in France, the largest proportion of the costs relate to agent's fees.

On the other hand, countries such as Denmark, Iceland or Slovakia have transaction costs amounting to around 2 per cent, most of which is accounted for by agent's fees.

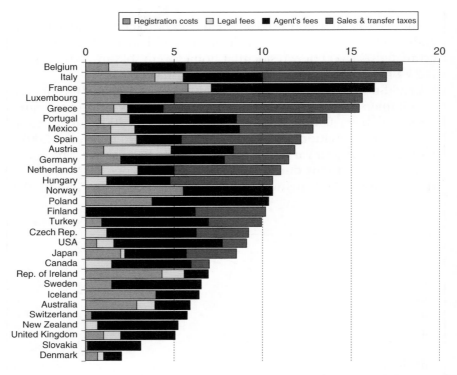

Figure 1.20   Transaction costs, selected countries, 2007 (percentage of the total value of the property)
Source: www.globalpropertyguide.com (accessed 28 December 2007).

Housing policies in Europe

Housing policies in Europe were not consistent before 1945. However, from 1945 onwards, specific policies began to emerge, originally driven by the effort to rebuild the towns and cities damaged during the Second World War (see Suárez *et al.*, 2005).

While housing policies usually pursue a common goal – to help citizens gain access to a decent home – they encompass a very broad range of actions. A division can be made between those policies implemented directly by the government – such as social housing, comprising rented dwellings owned by government agencies; and those that stimulate private activity.

The measures intended to motivate private initiatives in the desired direction can be in the form of a range of instruments: tax benefits, improved transparency and information, and subsidies. In their turn,

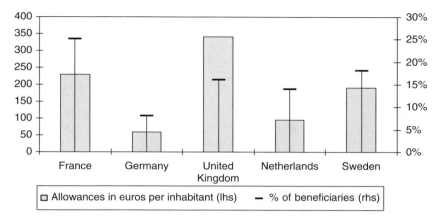

Figure 1.21 Housing subsidies, selected European countries, 2002–3 (allowance per inhabitant and percentage of beneficiaries)
Source: Fribourg (2002), cited in United Nations Economic Commission for Europe (2006) *Guidelines on Social Housing: Principles and Examples* (New York and Geneva: UN).

tax benefits and subsidies may target the producers of the dwellings that are sold and/or the owners of the dwellings that are rented (object subsidies or subsidies to brick and mortar), or the citizens who buy or rent the properties (subsidies to people or housing allowances).

General trends in European housing policies and the present situation

Housing policies vary enormously between one country and another. This is true for Western European countries, and even more so when the Central and Eastern European countries that have recently acquired EU membership are taken into account.

As a generalization, we can say that housing policies in Western Europe – particularly in Northern Europe – can be divided into three stages: 'recovery' immediately after 1945, when the focus was placed on reconstruction – supported by large subsidies and government finance – to provide social housing. In the second stage ('growing diversity'), up to 1970, the focus was on improving quality and including private ownership; here the national policies show greater divergence. In the third stage, from 1970 up to the time of writing, public spending has been reduced – initially because of the recessions of the 1970s and later because of political philosophy – and has become more market-driven (see Priemus *et al.*, 1993). See Figure 1.21 for an example of the diversity in the types of subsidies and their scope.

Table 1.15   Object and subject subsidies, selected countries, Europe and North America, 2006

		Object subsidies	
		Yes	None or very little
Housing allowance	Yes	EU countries (15 members)	Canada, Netherlands, Spain, USA
	No	Belgium, Luxembourg, Portugal	Greece

Source: United Nations Economic Commission for Europe (2006) *Guidelines on Social Housing: Principles and Examples* (New York and Geneva: UN).

There has been a shift in policies, from object subsidies to housing allowances (United Nations Economic Commission for Europe, 2006). Countries combine subsidies to people and to bricks and mortar in different proportions, although the general trend is towards a greater weight in subsidies to people, and a lower weighting in the subsidies targeting production; see Table 1.15.

There is a shift towards a larger proportion of owner-occupied dwellings – at least in Western Europe, a result in many cases of specific policies. In the EU-15, the percentage of owner-occupied houses increased from 57 per cent in 1980 to 65 per cent in 2004. Figure 1.22 shows all of the EU-15 countries where there has been a significant variation in the percentage of owner-occupied dwellings, defined here as a variation greater than 5 per cent (in either direction). (Note: The latest data on the owner-occupancy rate is included in Table 1.9; here the variation since the 1970s is addressed.) It can be seen that the proportion of owner-occupied houses has increased in all the countries listed.

By way of illustration of the main policies that have been implemented in Western European countries, and their most recent trends, the chapter closes with a brief review of the situation in those countries that are considered to have particularly characteristic housing policies. These are: Austria, Sweden, the United Kingdom, the Netherlands, Spain, France and Denmark, countries that pick up on the main trends in Western Europe: the implementation of the first systematic policies after the Second World War; diminishing coverage of policies in Northern Europe, where they reach more citizens than in Southern European countries; the increase in owner occupancy in most countries the increasing relevance of providing help to the citizens instead of to

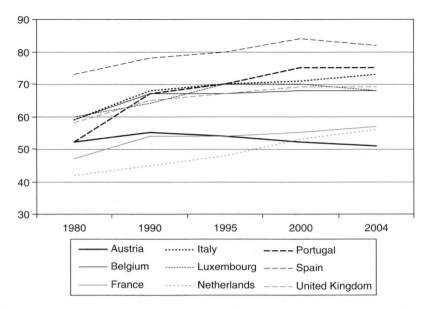

Figure 1.22 European countries with significant variation in the proportion of owner-occupied houses, 1980–2004

Note: Percentage of owner-occupied houses out of the total. A variation is considered to be significant when the percentage changes by more than 5 per cent between 1980 and 2004.

Source: Ministry of Infrastructure of the Italian Republic (2006) *Housing Statistics in the European Union, 2005/2006* (Federcasa, Italian Housing Federation, September).

bricks and mortar; and the decentralization of decision-making and the implementation of housing policies within countries. Housing policies differ among countries so the trends highlighted are those that are most common and not necessarily true for all.

Austria

Unlike other countries which have a more limited scope, Austria provides an extensive coverage to its citizens in its housing policies. In Vienna, 24 per cent of the inhabitants benefit from social housing. The limits restricting these housing allowances are very broad; it is considered that the public responsibility to assure adequate housing for citizens should not be left entirely to the free market (National Board of Housing Building and Planning, Sweden, and the Ministry for Regional Development, Czech Republic, 2004). Only 10–20 per cent of the population is not entitled to any type of subsidy (Amann, 2004).

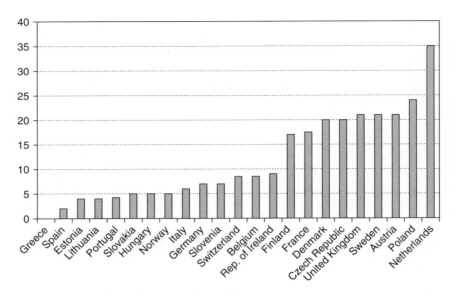

Figure 1.23   Share of social rental dwellings in the housing supply, Europe, c. year 2000
Source: United Nations Economic Commission for Europe (2006) *Guidelines on Social Housing: Principles and Examples* (New York and Geneva: UN, 2006).

Immediately after the Second World War there were no restrictions on allowances by income or type of dwelling. The first restriction was made in 1954, limiting allowances to dwellings of between $90\,m^2$ and $130\,m^2$, and in 1972, restrictions were introduced based on personal income (Donner, 2000).

Housing policy in Austria was centralized by the state until 1987–8, when all the central government's financing responsibilities were transferred to the nine provinces. Each province has a housing policy with its own instruments, although they concur in some aspects, such as on supply subsidies. Few responsibilities now remain at national level.

Austria chose to encourage rental as form of house occupancy and currently has one of the highest percentages of social housing; see Figure 1.23 (in addition to social rental properties, however, there is also accommodation that is privately rented). Since 1980, the percentage of households that rent their home has remained stable at between 40 per cent and 46 per cent, and social housing accounts for between 21 per cent and 26 per cent of the housing stock. The percentage of owner-occupied homes has increased slightly, to 57 per cent.

Not only are the citizens' rents subsidized, but subsidies and loans are also made available to builders; 80 per cent of new housing built is co-financed by the public sector, and it may be said that preference is given to production over the individual.

Sweden

Sweden's housing policy provides universal coverage, offering allowances for all types of occupancy. In 2002, 80 per cent of the families who rented their dwelling received benefits; 11 per cent of those who were members of co-operatives did so; and 9 per cent of homeowners (Lujanen, 2004). Rental has always been the favoured form of occupancy. Since 1980, the percentage of rented dwellings has varied between 38 per cent and 45 per cent. In 2004, social housing accounted for 22 per cent of the dwellings in Sweden.

During the 1960s, a plan was launched to promote housing production with special loans and subsidized interest rates. The extension of the plan in the 1970s and 1980s led to a large number of unoccupied dwellings. This, coupled with the economic recession, led to funds being shifted to loans to citizens, changing to a system based on subsidies to individuals.

The central government is responsible for both legislation and subsidies, while the municipal governments are responsible for designing and implementing the policies. In 2003, 1,592.4 million euros were allocated towards directing subsidies to meet housing demand, preference being given to families with children and to pensioners.

United Kingdom

The United Kingdom provides an intermediate level of citizen coverage. In 1980, funds were distributed roughly equally between subsidies for housing development (47 per cent) and to citizens (53 per cent); see Figure 1.24. However, as a result of policy changes, the proportions changed and, in 1995, 27 per cent was allocated to bricks and mortar and 73 per cent to individuals. Subsequently, the trend changed yet again and by 2004 the percentages were 40 per cent to bricks and mortar and 60 per cent to individuals (Wilcox, 2005).

The evolution of housing policies in the United Kingdom has been similar to those in other European countries, which started by focusing subsidies on production, consisting mainly of social housing. Britain had a high percentage of social rental accommodation until the 1980s, when a policy called 'right to buy' was introduced, which encouraged people to buy their own homes. As a result, the owner-occupied housing stock increased, together with an increase in subsidies to people. After

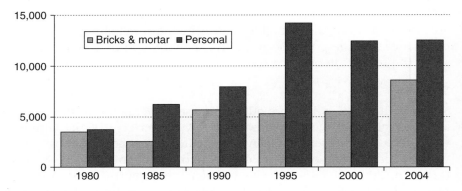

Figure 1.24 Subsidies to housing development and to citizens, United Kingdom, 1980–2004 (millions of pounds sterling, at 2002–3 prices)
Source: Wilcox (2005).

1980, the total number of rented dwellings fell, from 40.2 per cent to 29 per cent in 2004, and, within the segment of rented housing, the percentage of social housing fell from 28.9 per cent to 21 per cent during the same period. In 2005, owner-occupied dwellings accounted for 70 per cent of the total, as shown in Table 1.9 (see page 28).

Housing policy is centralized by the state. The Office of the Deputy Prime Minister is assisted by the Housing Corporation in regulating housing associations that are financed from public funds.

The Netherlands

The Netherlands has also opted to subsidize rental accommodation, dating from the measures taken at the end of the Second World War. Both subsidies to individuals and to suppliers were focused on this sector, consisting of rent allowances and subsidies or loans to those who supplied this sector. The proportion of rented housing fell from 56 per cent to 45 per cent between 1980 and 2004, and social rental has followed the same trend, decreasing from 39 per cent to 35 per cent. Owner-occupied dwellings accounted for 55 per cent of the total in 2004.

In 1989, a number of important changes took place. On the one hand, the policies were decentralized from a system in which housing finance, construction and administration was controlled by the government, to a privatization system that at the time of writing places the burden on housing associations. Another change was the shift of subsidies from production to individual citizens.

Spain

Spanish housing policies, which favour citizens with lower incomes, cover 12 per cent of the population. Housing policies were decentralized during the 1980s from the central government to the regions. However, the state still draws up plans for direct allowances for the purchase and restoration of dwellings, and these are administered by the regions through agreements between the two parties. In addition to the State Plan, the regions also devise their own housing plans. Assistance favours ownership over renting, and targets the individual. The measures include tax deductions, grants for first-time home buyers, and mortgage subsidies.

In 1960, 45 per cent of housing was rented; then a rent control system was introduced that led to a reduction in houses for rent; the system was moderated in 1985. By 1980, rented dwellings represented only 21 per cent of the total housing stock, and continued to fall, to 16 per cent by 2004. Social rental accounts for only 2 per cent of the total.

France

In France, 19.5 per cent of the population is covered by housing policies. French housing policy is centralized at the state level; only the financing is shared with local authorities. The state has been responsible for social housing since 1950 and, starting from that time, public funds were created for the construction of social dwellings. More than half of the funds (53 per cent) come from the state budget and the rest are drawn from the workers' social security contributions and from local authorities.

The proportion of rented dwellings in France has remained relatively stable since 1980 at about 38 per cent. In 2004, social housing accounted for 17 per cent of the total, and owner-occupied dwellings accounted for 54.2 per cent (see Table 1.9 on page 28).

The country occupies the middle ground in the distribution of subsidies between production and people. As with many other countries, France began by subsidizing house development. The first change was made in 1977, when subsidies to individuals were increased. By 1984, subsidies to bricks and mortar accounted for 49 per cent, compared with 34 per cent to individuals and 17 per cent given in the form of tax allowances. By 2002, subsidies to individuals had increased to 53 per cent of the total subsidies, with 20 per cent being allocated to bricks and mortar, and 27 per cent to tax allowances.

Denmark

In Denmark, housing is viewed as a necessary resource, and the state must guarantee this right. This explains the existence of an extensive level of coverage and the fact that 23 per cent of families in Denmark receive subsidies (National Board of Housing Building and Planning, Sweden, and the Ministry for Regional Development, Czech Republic, 2004). Of these families, 94 per cent live in rented dwellings, 5 per cent are members of housing co-operatives and 1 per cent are owner-occupiers (these data for beneficiary families by type of occupancy are from 2002). Both the private and public rental sectors receive subsidies totalling more than half of the rental price.

Since 1980, the total rental stock has fluctuated between 40 per cent (2004) and 45 per cent (2005). In 2004, social housing accounted for 20 per cent of the total, and in 2006, 55 per cent of the houses were owner-occupied (see Table 1.9 on page 28).

Bibliography

Amann, W. (2005) 'The Austrian System of Social Housing Finance', Presentation at the European Real Estate Society Conference, Dublin (June).

Donner, C. (2000) *Housing Policies in the European Union: Theory and Practice.* Published by the author: Dr Christian Donner, Schlimekgasse 15, A-1238 Vienna.

European Mortgage Federation (2007) *Hypostat 2006* (November).

Eurostat (http://epp.eurostat.ec.europa.eu).

Long, M. (2007) 'UK Residential Property Market Overview', Presentation at the IPD European Investment Residential Conference.

Lujanen, M. (2004) *Housing and Housing Policy in the Nordic Countries*, Copenhagen: Nordic Council of Ministers.

Ministry of Employment of Spain (2006) *Elderly People in Spain: Report.*

Ministry of Infrastructure of the Italian Republic (2006) *Housing Statistics in the European Union, 2005/2006* (Federcasa, Italian Housing Federation, September).

National Board of Housing Building and Planning, Sweden, and the Ministry for Regional Development, Czech Republic (2004) *Housing Statistics in the European Union.*

OECD (2005) *Economic Outlook No. 78*, November.

Office of Federal Housing Enterprise Oversight House Price Index (OFHEO HPI) (http://www.ofheo.gov/HPI.aspx).

Priemus, H., Kleinman, M., Maclennan, D. and Turner B. (1993) *European Monetary, Economic and Political Union: Consequences for National Housing Policies, Housing and Urban Policy Studies*, No. 6 (Delft: Delft University Press).

Suárez, José Luis, Vassallo, Amparo and Muñoz, Natalia (2005) 'Hogar, dulce hogar. Análisis de las políticas de vivienda de los Países Bajos, Suecia, Austria, Reino Unido y España', *IESE Alumni Review* (April–June).

United Nations (2007) *World Population Prospects: The 2006 Revision* (New York, UN).

United Nations Economic Commission for Europe (UNECE) (2006a) *Bulletin of Housing Statistics for Europe and North America* (New York and Geneva: UN).

United Nations Economic Commission for Europe (UNECE) (2006b) *Guidelines on Social Housing: Principles and Examples* (New York and Geneva: UN).

Wilcox, S. (2005) *More Apparent than Real? The Decline of Bricks and Mortar Subsidies* (York: University of York).

Website

www.globalpropertyguide.com (accessed 28 December 2007 and 11 January 2008).

2
Commercial Real Estate

From an economic point of view, urban real estate property can be classified as:

- *Owner-occupied houses*. These assets could be and in fact are the object of buying and selling transactions, but in markets characterized by high atomization and low transparency.
- *Commercial real estate*. These properties are traded more frequently, principally by companies or other professional entities. They usually have well-established investment and rental markets.
- *Special real estate assets*. These include all other types – usually property with a very low or non-existent turnover of ownership, such as churches, public buildings or facilities, and so on.

Commercial real estate includes many diverse assets. The main properties, by value and frequency of transaction, are offices, retail, and industrial and logistics, but this category also includes hotels, apartment blocks, parking places, retirement homes and so on. Commercial real estate and a portion of the housing market (rented houses) together comprise the investment prospects for institutional investors.

This chapter will deal with offices, shopping centres (a category within retail properties) and industrial property (including logistics). The information presented will include mainly data provided by real estate agencies since, given their high transaction frequency and elevated individual value, these assets comprise the main activity of that industry. It should be borne in mind that, when talking about commercial real estate it is more common to refer to cities rather than countries. In this field, in most cases the available information is confined to the main cities, so in each case the cities with most widely available data have been included.

Following the downturn perceived in certain countries and the financial squeeze of the second part of 2007 and early 2008, there is a fear of a slowdown in the activity levels of commercial real estate. Some data on the very recent development of the office market for the City of London, a qualified witness to this impact, are offered. Although the overall figures for the year 2007 have not been negative, a slowdown during last quarter is very apparent.

Given their long-term nature, properties are often bought, sold or rented several times during their lives. When talking about each type of activity, we shall first establish the size of the stock (floor space and its variations), then the rental market and its principal economic variables (take-up, rents, occupancy), and finally, the investment market (transactions, prices, yield). Yield is the immediate profitability from a property, measured as the ratio of net income to property price, where net income is rent minus expenses incurred by the owner.

The European commercial real estate stock and markets

Existing property stock, measured by floor space or investment value, may be regarded in three different ways. One of them is simply the total stock constructed and extant. Another category is represented by those properties that may readily be the object of an economic transaction, and which are a subset of the first; and finally, again a subset of the previous one, all the property that is already in the hands of identifiable investors, usually institutions. These last two are the most relevant to an economic study, and may be called 'investible' and 'invested' stock, respectively(see RREEF Research, 2007: 2).

In 2006, Europe was the continent with the second-largest real estate stock after North America, with an investible stock of 6.1 trillion US dollars and, as may be expected, the majority of that was in Western Europe. The total invested was 3.2 trillion US dollars, a third of the global total (see Figure 2.1). Asia is the region in third place.

Among the thirteen largest markets in the world, in terms of investible commercial real estate volume, there are five European countries; these are Germany, the United Kingdom, France, Italy and the Netherlands (see Table 2.1). The largest markets are found in the USA and Japan. The largest expected increase in the near future (the period 2006–11), is expected in Brazil, Russia, India and China (the BRIC countries).

As stated earlier, in dealing with commercial real estate, two markets can be identified. One is the rental market; and the other, the investment market. Since the mid-1990s, investment volume and prices have increased significantly in the European real estate markets. The

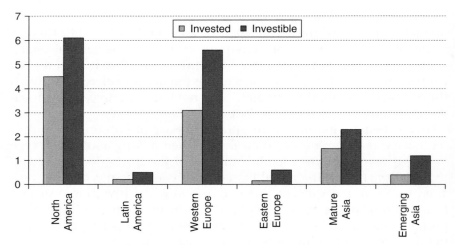

Figure 2.1 Global real estate stock value, 2006 (trillions of US dollars)
Source: RREEF Research (2007) *The Future Size of the Global Real Estate Market* (July): 3.

Table 2.1 Investible commercial real estate stock, top ten countries globally, 2006 and forecast growth 2006–11 (billions of US dollars)

Country	2006	Growth 2006–11	Percentage change
USA	4,250	1,350	31
Japan	1,200	500	41
Germany	800	300	37
United Kingdom	790	110	14
France	400	150	37
Canada	250	100	50
Italy	250	50	20
Australia	200	50	25
Netherlands	170	66	38
China	168	522	310
Brazil	43	57	135
Russia	35	65	190
India	11	39	350

Source: RREEF Research (2007) *The Future Size of the Global Real Estate Market* (July): 1.

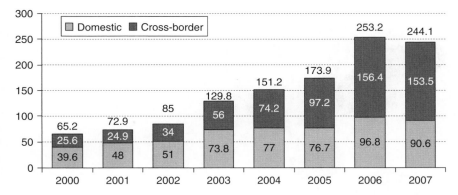

Figure 2.2   Direct real estate investment volume, Europe, 2000–7 (billions of euros)
Source: Jones Lang LaSalle (personal correspondence with the author).

industry's positive returns and low correlation with equity and fixed income investment, combined with enhanced market accessibility, have encouraged many investors to increase the weight of real estate assets in their investment portfolios. Transactions were rampant in 2006, reaching 253.2 billion euros (45.6 per cent up on 2005), but slowed down slightly in 2007 to 244.1 billion euros (4 per cent lower than in 2006); see Figure 2.2.

In 2007, the 'Big Three' European markets (the United Kingdom, Germany and France) continued to dominate European investment. In France, this volume grew by 25 per cent and in Germany by 6 per cent, while in the United Kingdom it decreased by 22 per cent. Other markets registering growth in 2007 were Spain (54 per cent), the Netherlands (23 per cent), and Belgium (6 per cent) (Jones Lang LaSalle, *European Capital Markets Bulletin*, 2007).

One of the factors contributing to the expansion of the real estate market before 2006 was the development of private indirect property investment vehicles. These gave investors access to specialized management and new markets, while also offering them the opportunity to participate in the development of large real estate projects (the primary vehicles for indirect real estate investment are presented in Chapter 4). In contrast, as mentioned previously, 2007 has registered a fall in investment volume because less liquidity was observed in the real estate markets prompted by the financial turmoil observed in the second half of the year. The geographical diversification policies of development companies has also contributed to cross-border transactions.

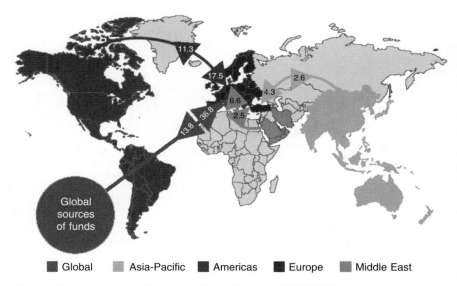

Figure 2.3   Inter-regional capital flows, Europe, 2007 (billions of euros)
Source: Jones Lang LaSalle (personal correspondence with the author).

The cross-border investment data appear in Figure 2.2. The cross-border transaction volume increased from 2000 to 2006 but showed a minor decrease in 2007. In 2005, of a total 173.9 billion euros invested, 97.2 billion were cross-border. In 2006, of the transactions totalling 253.2 billion euros, 156.4 billion were cross border, a 61 per cent increase over 2005. Foreign investment in 2006 represented 62 per cent of the total, up from 56 per cent in 2005. In the same way, during 2007, the cross-border percentage over total volume remained strong (63 per cent) (Jones Lang LaSalle, *European Capital Markets Bulletin*, 2007).

'Cross-border', applies when the origin of the funds is different from the place where the assets are allocated. Considering Europe, this can occur either with funds proceeding from another continent, or in transactions from one country to another within the European frontiers. The former are 'inter-regional' transactions and the latter are 'intra-regional' ones.

In 2007, the inter-regional investment in Europe – inflow from another regions – reached 65.2 billion euros and was the key factor in the increase in European cross-border activity to 153.5 billion euros. Out of that investment, 36.8 billion euros came from global sources, 17.5 billion from America, 4.3 billion from the Asia-Pacific area, and 6.6 billion from the Middle East. Global sources refer to vehicles with multinational funding; see Figure 2.3. When the outflow of 30.2 billion

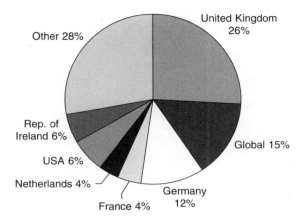

Figure 2.4 Sources of capital invested in European real estate, 2007 (percentages of the total)
Source: Jones Lang LaSalle (personal correspondence with the author).

euros is deducted from that inflow, an inter-regional net investment of 35 billion euros remains in 2007.

Concerning the specific origins and destinations of the investment in Europe, during 2007 the principal source of funds for real estate investment was the United Kingdom, accounting for 26 per cent of the total; see Figure 2.4. The next sources of funds in importance are Germany, America, and Ireland, while 15 per cent of the total investment has a global origin.

The United Kingdom is also the principal destination of investment capital, with 30 per cent of the total; see Figure 2.5. Behind the United Kingdom come Germany and France, and these three markets account for 63 per cent of the total investment in Europe.

Offices

Offices are the most characteristic investment assets of commercial real estate, because of the whole size of the sector, their liquidity, and because they are easier to manage, usually requiring relatively little effort to rent and typically attracting good-quality tenants. Figure 2.6 shows offices as the predominant sector within the commercial real estate.

Office space available

The amount of floor space dedicated to offices in Europe varies greatly from one city to another, depending on the importance of the area in

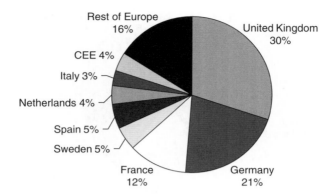

Figure 2.5   Destination of capital invested in European real estate, 2007 (percentages)

Source: Jones Lang LaSalle (personal correspondence with the author).

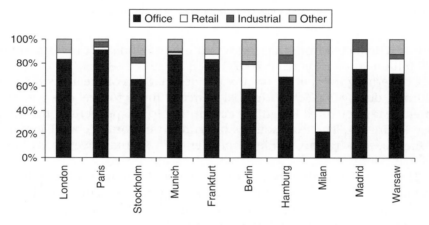

Figure 2.6   Top ten European cities, investment by sectors, 2006 (percentages of the total)

Source: CB Richard Ellis (2006) *European Investment Market View*: 4.

relation to the general economy of the country, the existing space available, the urban design or layout, and the regulations existing in each market. At the end of 2006, the most important market in Europe was Paris, with office space of almost 49 million m2. Central Paris, which includes Paris CBD, West CBD, Rive Gauche and Saint-Denis, accounts for 17.5 million m^2. The second biggest market was London, with 19.2 million m^2, where the centre (the City, the West End, Midtown (Holborn) and the South Bank) boasts 17.5 million m^2, mainly banking and financial services together with multinationals; see Figure 2.7.

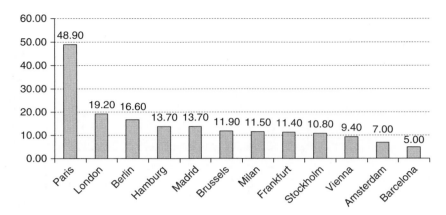

Figure 2.7 Office stock, principal European cities, third quarter, 2006 (millions of m²)
Source: Jones Lang Lasalle (personal correspondence with the author).

In Spain, the principal markets are Madrid and Barcelona. Madrid has 13.7 million m² of office space (the majority of it outside the centre), and its importance extends as far as Latin-American economies. Barcelona, on the other hand, is much smaller, with barely 5 million m² of office space, occupied principally by technology and design multinationals.

Brussels, with almost 12 million m², is a very important market, not only for the Belgian economy, but also because it is the location of various institutions of the European Union. Amsterdam, by contrast, has only 7 million m² available because of space constraints, despite its importance as a base for some technological, financial and publicity companies.

Frankfurt is also a significant city, as the headquarters of the European Central Bank as well as many German banks, and has 11.4 million m² dedicated to office space.

Another example of a market with small dimensions but high relevance is Vienna, with 9.4 million m²; it is the city of choice for many multinationals with operations in Central and Eastern Europe, as well as accommodating offices of the UN and the OPEC. The majority of business activity is based in the centre, as there are better service and transport conditions there.

Office development

To keep pace with the demands of economic evolution, the office space within cities is constantly expanding. Nevertheless, Paris, London and

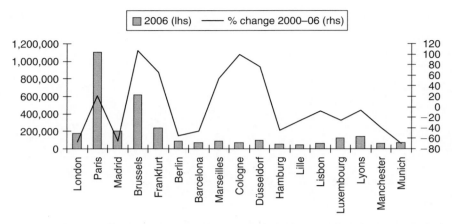

Figure 2.8   Office completions, selected European cities, 2006, and evolution 2000–6 (000s m² and percentage change)

Note: In the case of Marseilles, Lille and Lyons, data given are for 2005 as 2006 figures were not available. For Berlin and Cologne, the percentage change was calculated using 2001 data, as 2000 figures were not available. For the same reasons, 2002 data have been used for Luxembourg.

Source: Atisreal (2007) *European Office Markets*: 8–43.

Madrid have all reduced the number of new offices constructed since 2004. In Paris, during the period 2002–04, office space increased by approximately 1 million m² annually, but in 2005 this went down to some 800,000 m². In 2006, there was a slight increase, to just over 1 million m², but the forecast is for further reduction (this information, and much of the rest in this section, is from Atisreal (2007) *European Office Markets*: 8–40).

London's office space reduced from 600,000 m² in 2004 to 233,000 in 2005, and to less than 200,000 in 2006, but in 2007 there was an increase of 14 per cent, the first increase since the end of 2004. Madrid showed a decrease for four consecutive years, and fell to 200,000 m² in 2006; see Figure 2.8.

The challenge in Frankfurt is the lack of space in which to build, and for this reason the amount of new office space has decreased considerably each year. The year with the most activity was 2003, with 600,000 m² constructed. In Brussels, in 2006, there were 600,000 m² of new office space – almost a 50 per cent increase on the previous year.

Barcelona has seen an average of 150,000 m² of new office space annually, while in Berlin in 2006 the amount constructed was some 100,000 m² more than in the previous year. Certain cities are renovating specific areas and converting some buildings into offices. This is

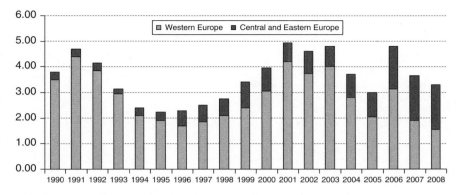

Figure 2.9 Office completions, Europe, 1990–2008 (millions m²)
Note: Data for 2006 are estimations; 2007 and 2008 are forecasts.
Source: Jones Lang LaSalle (2006/07) *Office Supply Pipeline in Europe*: 1.

the case in Barcelona's '22@' District, which was previously a depressed residential and industrial area.

The number of total office completions peaked in 2001 then decreased over 2005, but 2006 witnessed a recovery in the space put on to the market. The breakdown in Figure 2.9 between Western Europe and Central and Eastern Europe (CEE) stresses the growing importance of CEE.

Rental markets: occupation

The demand for office space has been increasing since 1992, with the exception of 2002 and 2003; see Figure 2.10. From 1991 to 2006, take-up increased more than 100 per cent, while gross domestic product (GDP) grew by about 27 per cent. The peak was in the year 2000, when take-up reached 10.9 million m². From 2002 to 2005 in Europe, annual take-up increased by 2 per cent, and in 2006, 9.2 million m² were transacted in main European cities, an increase of 15 per cent on the previous year, and the best result since the 2000 peak (Atisreal (2006) *Europe Quarterly-Office* (Q4): 2).

During the period 1991–2005, the biggest increases were in Barcelona, Madrid and Paris (380 per cent, 236 per cent and 145 per cent, respectively). In 2005 and 2006, the cities with the highest take-up levels were Paris, Central London and Madrid, followed by Munich, Brussels and Frankfurt (Atisreal, 2006). In 2006, the cities with the biggest year-on-year increase in take-up were Luxembourg (41.8 per cent), Inner Paris (31.4 per cent) and Berlin (26.3 per cent); see Figure 2.11.

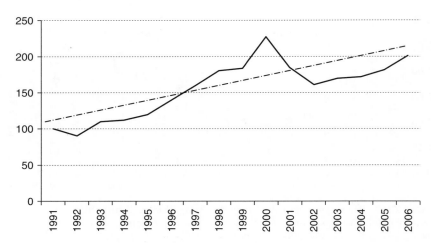

Figure 2.10   Take-up index, EU-15, 1991–2006 (index base 100 = 1991)
Note: Dotted line indicates trend.
Source: King Sturge (2006) *European Office Property Markets*: 5.

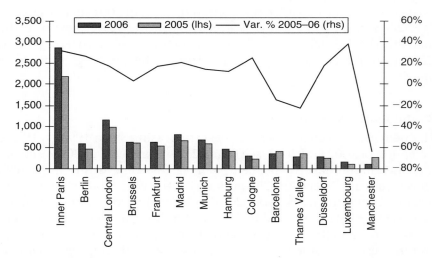

Figure 2.11   Take-up levels in the European market, 2005 and 2006 (000s m^2)
Source: Atisreal (2006) *Europe Quarterly Office Markets* (Q4): 1.

Prices

After 1994, the rental price of offices in the EU-15 increased steadily, until the third quarter of 2001, when prices reached a maximum value of 259 on the EU-15 index, where a value of 100 corresponds to the

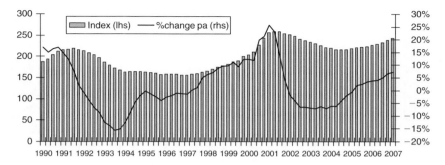

Figure 2.12 Rent variation, EU-15, 1990–2007 (quarterly value of the index with base 100 in 1986; annual percentage change)
Source: CB Richard Ellis (personal correspondence with the author).

prices in the year 1986. From the fourth quarter of 2001 until 2004, rental values decreased, to an index value of 217 points. From 2004 until the first quarter of 2007, rents grew at an annual rate of between 2 per cent and 7.2 per cent, with this last figure being for the latest period analysed; see Figure 2.12.

At the end of 2006, the cities with rents above 500 euros per m² were London (London West at 1500 euros per m² per year), Moscow (913 euros per m²), Paris (730 euros per m²) and Dublin (646 euros per m²). The three cities with the highest sub-500 euros values were Milan, Edinburgh and Stockholm. The cities with rents below 250 euros per m² per year were Berlin and Vienna (246 euros), Lisbon, Lyons and Prague (240 euros), while in last place was Budapest (222 euros); see Figure 2.13.

The four capitals with the greatest variation in rental prices across 2005 and 2006 were Oslo, London, Madrid and Dublin, which varied by more than 26 per cent. By contrast, Milan, Berlin and Budapest did not change. The rest of the capitals varied by between 1.5 per cent (Amsterdam) and 20 per cent (Moscow).

Vacancy rate

From its peak in 1993 the vacancy rate of 9 per cent dropped to a historical low in the year 2000, but three years later it was back above the 1993 peak. During 2005, it was 8.9 per cent, a drop from 2004. At the end of 2006, the average vacancy rate in Western Europe was 8.2 per cent, and 7.2 per cent in Eastern Europe (King Sturge (2007) *European Office Property Markets*: 2).

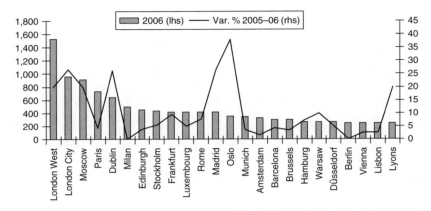

Figure 2.13   Rents in main European cities, 2006 (euros per m² and annual variation)

Source: Jones Lang LaSalle (2006) *European Office Property Clock* (4Q): 3.

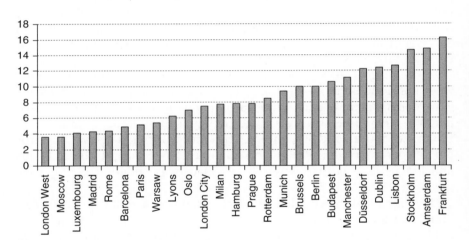

Figure 2.14   Office vacancy rate, main European cities, 2006 (percentages)

Source: Jones Lang LaSalle (2007) *Office Leasing Market Conditions in Europe* (March): 2–3.

Office vacancy varies greatly from city to city. In 2006, the three cities with the lowest vacancy rates were London West and Moscow, with 3.6 per cent, and Luxembourg, with 4.1 per cent. Madrid and Rome were in fourth and fifth place, with 4.3 per cent and 4.9 per cent, respectively; see Figure 2.14.

Frankfurt, Amsterdam and Stockholm have the highest vacancy rates in Europe, with 16.2 per cent, 14.8 per cent and 14.6 per cent,

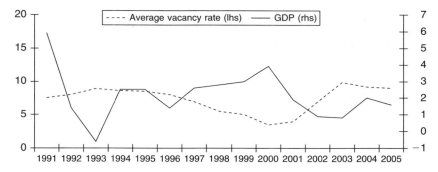

Figure 2.15　Office vacancy rate and GDP growth in the Euro Zone, 1991–2005 (percentages)

Source: King Sturge (2005) *European Office Property Markets*: 4.

respectively, more than 10 percentage points above the capitals with the lowest rates.

Even within the same city we can find important differences between the financial centre and the suburbs, as with London (10 per cent in the City compared to 6.5 per cent in the West End), Madrid (with a much higher vacancy rate in the suburbs), and Paris (7.4 per cent in La Défense, 4.9 per cent in the centre and 3.1 per cent in the suburbs).

The vacancy rate depends on the net take-up (gross take-up minus freed-up office space), and on the existing supply and new constructions. This was the case in Barcelona, where the few new offices and the increase in take-up combined to improve the vacancy rate, which fell in 2005 to 6.3 per cent.

Given that the take-up depends on the level of general economic activity, a correlation between vacancy rates and GDP can be expected. The comparison of these variables is shown in Figure 2.15, where we can observe an inversely-proportional trend. In fact, from 2000 to 2004, there was a particularly marked decline in GDP growth and a simultaneous increase in the vacancy rate.

Investment market: volume and yields

The office sector is the principal area of investment in commercial real estate. In 2006, it represented 50 per cent of the total volume, 7 per cent higher than 2005. In cities such as London, Paris, Brussels or Luxembourg, more than 80 per cent of the real estate investment was in this sector. By contrast, in Berlin, Barcelona, Cologne and Lyons, less than 50 per cent of real estate investment was in offices, for a total of less

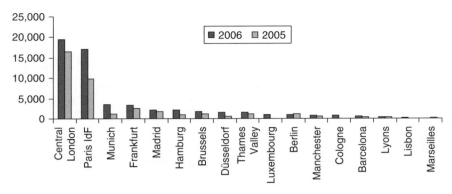

Figure 2.16   Office investment market, selected European cities, 2005 and 2006 (millions of euros)
Source: Atisreal (2005–2006) *European Office Market in Perspective*: 5.

than 5 billion euros. Moscow devoted 6 per cent, and 30 per cent of its total investment in 2005 and 2006, respectively, to offices.

London and Paris had the greatest investment in offices in 2006 – almost 20 billion euros; see Figure 2.16. This represents an increase of 17 per cent for London, and 75 per cent for Paris, over 2005. The largest annual investment increase was 199 per cent in Munich, with 1.2 billion euros in 2005 and 3.6 billion euros in 2006. Hamburg and Düsseldorf also saw large increases, of 40 per cent and 125 per cent, respectively.

When looking at international diversification in European markets, either from outside Europe or from one European country to another, it could be natural to target, in the first place, the prime zones of the largest and most consolidated markets. However, the liquidity that was experienced in the period before mid-2006, and the relatively small asset offering in those zones, have led investors to consider second-level zones in the principal markets, or even in other cities of lesser importance (secondary markets) when seeking higher yields. The availability of assets for investment and the search for better returns have also led investors to look towards Central and Eastern Europe in the recent years.

In 2006, yields decreased in all the cities studied, apart from Brussels and Lille, where they remained stable. The sharpest fall was in Lyons (0.7 per cent), followed by Madrid and Berlin with 0.6 per cent, and London at the bottom of the list with 0.5 per cent. There was a general convergence towards yields of 5.5 per cent across all office markets.

At the end of 2007, the lowest prime investment yields in Europe were, from minor to major, those in Dublin and Paris (around 4 per cent),

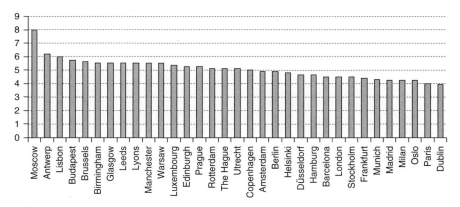

Figure 2.17 Prime office yields, main European cities, 2007 (percentages)
Source: Jones Lang LaSalle (2007) *Key Market Indicators* (4Q): 2.

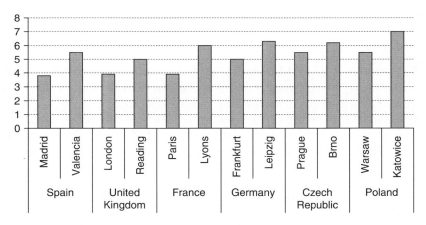

Figure 2.18 Prime office yields, primary versus secondary cities, selected European countries, Summer 2007 (percentages)
Note: There are small differences between the yields shown in Figure 2.18 and those in Figure 2.17 because of the difference in source data.
Source: Knight Frank (2007) *European Investment Commentary* (Summer): 5.

followed by Oslo, Milan and Madrid. In contrast, the highest yields were to be found in Moscow, Antwerp, Lisbon and Budapest; see Figure 2.17.

As mentioned earlier, it is possible to find higher yields in secondary markets in the relevant countries, or in cities within less-consolidated countries; see Figure 2.18. Paradoxically, the interest shown by investors in these secondary cities has caused a narrowing of the spread between their yields and those of the principal cities.

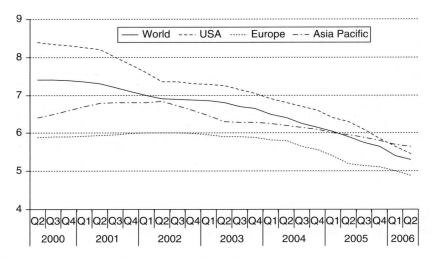

Figure 2.19   Global office prime yields, 2000–6
Source: RREEF, NREI, CB Richard Ellis, Jones Lang LaSalle.

The search for profitable investment has increased in Central and Eastern Europe, in cities such as Krakow or Katowice in the East, and smaller Central European cities such as Vienna and Zürich.

The yield compression in Europe referred to earlier is part of a global phenomenon, as can be seen from Figure 2.19. The search for higher yields in less developed markets provoked the narrowing of margins across regions. The prime yields across the different continents have evolved from fairly distant levels in 2000, to all of them almost converging within a range of less than one percentage point in 2006.

The situation in the London office market at the end of 2007.

There were signs of a slowdown in the London office market in the final quarter of 2007. Occupier confidence to commit appeared diminished, and the take up level had decreased in all submarkets (apart from in city centres), resulting in only around 241500 m^2 leased during the last quarter of 2007 (the lowest level for nearly three years and around a 30 per cent less than in the third quarter of the year); see Figure 2.20.

Nevertheless, rents have continued to grow, driven by the strength of the West End submarket, but at a slower pace compared to the last two quarters of the year (only 1.8 per cent of growth compared with 2.6 per cent for Q3, and 6.9 per cent for Q2); see Figure 2.21.

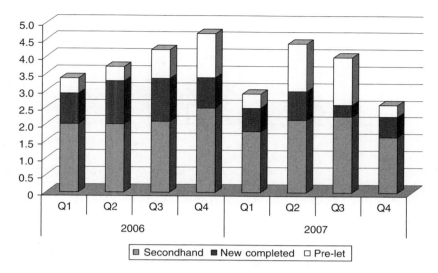

Figure 2.20 Central London office market take-up, 2006 and 2007 (millions sq. ft)

Note: Most data in this section are taken from CB Richard Ellis (2007) *Central London Offices* (Q4), unless another reference is quoted.

Source: CB Richard Ellis, *Central London Offices Market View* (Q4 2007). P.2.

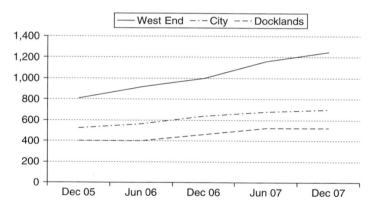

Figure 2.21 Prime rents, main submarkets, London, 2006–7 (pounds sterling per m^2)

Source: Jones Lang LaSalle (2007) *Central London Market Report* (Q4): 4.

The effects of the credit squeeze are also apparent in the investment arena. Despite the total 2007 investment volume being the highest recorded, (18.7 billion pounds sterling traded, mainly driven by Docklands (Jones Lang LaSalle (2007) *Central London Market Report*

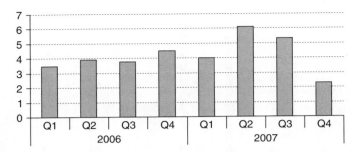

Figure 2.22   Central London investment transactions, 2006 and 2007 (billions of pounds sterling)
Source: CB Richard Ellis (2007) *Central London Offices Market View* (Q4): 10.

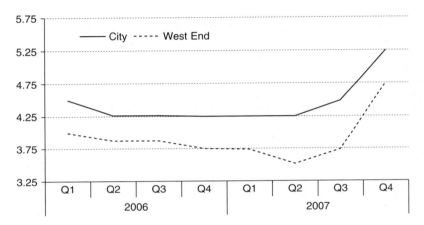

Figure 2.23   City and West End prime yields, London, 2006 and 2007 (percentages)
Source: CB Richard Ellis (2007) *Central London Offices Market View* (Q4): 10.

(Q4)), this cannot disguise the fact that activity fell to 2.3 billion pounds sterling in the last quarter, the lowest quarterly total since 2005, and representing 49 per cent less than the same period last year; see Figure 2.22.

These events has resulted in rising yields, up to 150 basis points higher than the third quarter in the West End, and 125 basis points higher than the same quarter in the City. This change has been perceived as the promise of a more liquid market, and so has alerted buyers to search for opportunities in Central London; see Figure 2.23.

Table 2.2 Shopping centre classification

Format	Type of scheme		Gross leasable area (GLA)(sq. m)
Traditional	Very large		80,000 and above
	Large		40,000–79,999
	Medium		20,000–39,999
	Small	Comparison-based	5,000–19,999
		Convenience-based	5,000–19,999
Specialized	Retail park	Large	20,000 and above
		Medium	10,000–19,999
		Small	5,000–9,999
	Factory outlet centre		5,000 and above
	Theme-orientated	Leisure-based	5,000 and above
	centre	Non-leisure-based	5,000 and above

Source: Lambert (2006): 35.

Shopping centres

In 2005 the International Council of Shopping Centres (ICSC) published a pan-European standard for classifying shopping centres to facilitate cross-border comparison and foster transparency in the sector. According to this standard, a shopping centre is 'a retail property that is planned, built and managed as a single entity, comprising units and "communal" areas, with a minimum gross leasable area (GLA) of 5,000 square meters (sq. m) (International Council of Shopping Centres, 2005).

This new standard classifies shopping centres into eleven types, which are in turn grouped in two broader categories: traditional and specialized. The former is an all-purpose scheme, which may be either enclosed or open-air, while the latter includes specific purpose-built retail schemes that are typically open-air. Both traditional and specialized centres may be further classified by size and other criteria, as can be seen from Table 2.2.

Within the small traditional centres, the comparison-based ones, include retailers, typically sell fashion apparel and shoes, home furnishings, electronics and toys; whereas the convenience-based ones sell essential goods (supermarkets and hypermarkets, for example).

Among the specialized shopping centres, the retail parks tend to have one or more specialist retailers – IKEA, for example; factory outlet centres have separate store units where manufacturers and retailers sell

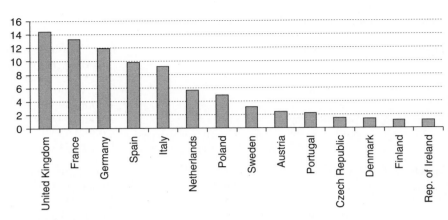

Figure 2.24   Shopping centre stock, Europe, 2006 (millions m² GLA)
Source: Spanish Association of Shopping Centres.

merchandise at discounted prices; and theme-orientated centres can be either leisure-based (usually with a cinema, bowling alley and so on), or non-leisure-based (concentrating on a niche market for fashion/apparel or home furnishings, or targeting specific customers, such as passengers at airports).

Total shopping centre space available

The European shopping centre market has grown in recent years. At the time of writing, it consists of 90 million m² of GLA of shopping centres, and it reached around 100 million m² by the end of 2007. The United Kingdom has the largest stock, with 14 million m². Next is France, with a stock of 13 million m², in third place is Germany, with more than 11 million m², and in fourth place is Spain, with nearly 10 million m². Together, these four countries account for 52 per cent of the European shopping centre market. The EU-15 as a whole accounts for 80 per cent of the total stock of shopping centres in Europe, and the EU-25 represents 89 per cent; see Figure 2.24.

With regard to density, in Europe as a whole, the average shopping centre area per 1,000 inhabitants in 2006 was 189.7 m², and in EU-27 this figure amounts to 176 m²; see Figure 2.25. Norway (not shown) heads the European shopping centre density ranking, with 797 m² per 1,000 inhabitants. Next are Sweden and the Netherlands, with 335 m² per 1,000 inhabitants. Countries such as the Czech Republic, Poland

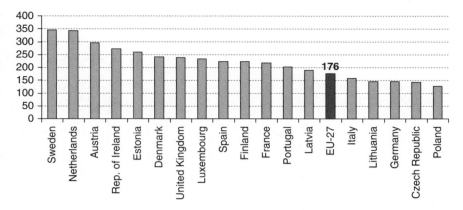

Figure 2.25 Shopping centre density, Europe, 2006 (GLA in m² per 1,000 inhabitants)
Source: Spanish Association of Shopping Centres.

and Belgium have the lowest density among the countries studied, with 131.7, 110.9 and 96.7 m² per 1,000 inhabitants, respectively.

Evolution

Shopping-centre growth has been fairly constant since 1980, with small declines in some years. During 2006, around 9 million m² of new shopping centre space was constructed; see Figure 2.26.

In recent years there has been a sharp increase in shopping centre development in Central and Eastern Europe, with Russia and Poland having had the fastest growth in shopping centre space during 2006; in fact, in Russia, almost 90 per cent of the existing stock has been completed since 2002. In Central Europe, the corresponding figure is 35–70 per cent, and in Western Europe 10–20 per cent. All countries in CEE apart from Estonia are below the EU-25 average, so it is clear that they still have considerable potential for growth in the sector.

Turning to shopping centres in the construction pipeline, in 2006–07 Spain headed the ranking with more than 2 million m² under construction, more or less on a par with Italy; see Figure 2.27. Looking towards the future, the country forecast to have the greatest amount of construction in 2007–08 is Russia, with more than 4 million m², followed by Turkey and Italy with around 2.2 million m² each; and at some distance behind them are Poland, Spain and Germany. The United Kingdom is in seventh place with just under than 1.7 million m² of new centres under construction. These figures reveal the increasing importance of some

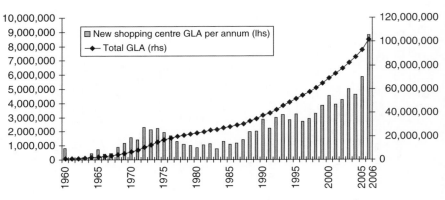

Figure 2.26 Shopping centre growth, Europe, 1960–2006 (in m^2)
Source: Cushman and Wakefield (2007): 3.

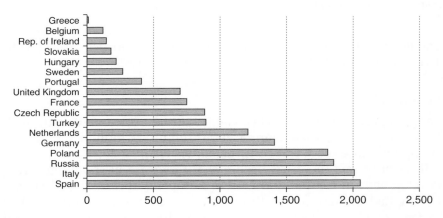

Figure 2.27 Shopping centres under construction, Europe, 2006–7 (GLA in 000s m^2)
Source: Jones Lang LaSalle Shopping (2006) *Centre Development Goes from Strength to Strength*: 1.

emerging markets in Central and Eastern Europe (Jones Lang LaSalle (2007) *Shopping Centre Development – The Boom Goes On*: 2).

Rental markets: prices

The United Kingdom is the European country with the highest rents in shopping centres. In 2006, the rents there went up to between 2,500 and 2,800 euros per m^2 per year. In second and third place are France and the

Table 2.3 Shopping centre rents, European prime zones, April 2006 (euros/ m^2/year)

	Prime rent (€/m^2/year)
United Kingdom	2,500–2,800
France	1,500–1,800
Republic of Ireland	1,500–1,800
Belgium	1,000–1,100
Portugal	800–900
Finland	800–900
Spain	700–850
Italy	650–750
Hungary	600–1,000
Poland	600–1,000
Turkey	600–700
Netherlands	600–700
Sweden	550–750
Germany	550–650
Denmark	450–550
Czech Republic	400–600

Source: Cushman and Wakefield (2006) *European Pipeline for 2006/2007* (April): 3.

Republic of Ireland, with 1,500–1,800 euros per m^2 per year, followed by Belgium with 1,000–1,100 euros per m^2 per year. Countries with the lowest shopping centre rents, such as Turkey (600–700 euros per m^2 per year), Poland and the Czech Republic (400–600 euros per m^2 per year), also have the highest rates of return (8.50–10 per cent, 6.50–7 per cent and 6.50–6.75 per cent, respectively); see Table 2.3.

Investment market: volume

Shopping centre investment is very strong, and continues to grow; see Figure 2.28. In 2006 in Europe, the total volume of investment transactions in the shopping centre market was 26 billion euros. The United Kingdom has had the largest and most active market for years but, despite this, the volume of transactions there dropped from 11 billion euros in 2005 to 8 billion in 2006 (King Sturge (2008) *European Retail Property: Looking beyond the Benign* (2008): 3).

The decrease in investment in the United Kingdom is a result of the increasing price of assets, which has favoured the increase in other national markets. Germany is the principal beneficiary of this shift,

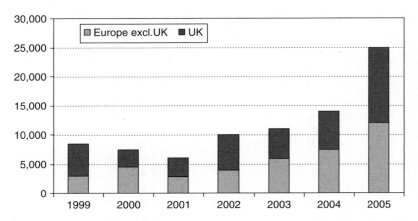

Figure 2.28   European shopping centre investment transactions, 1999–2005 (millions of euros)

Source: CB Richard Ellis (2006) *EU Shopping Centre Investment*: 2.

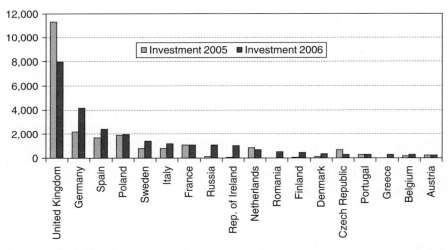

Figure 2.29   European shopping centre investment transactions, by country, 2005 and 2006 (millions of euros)

Source: CBRE, Property Data and King Sturge.

with an investment level of 4.2 billion euros in 2006 – double that of the previous year. Investors are also heading to Eastern Europe. Other countries with high capital growth in Western Europe are the Republic of Ireland and Spain; see Figure 2.29.

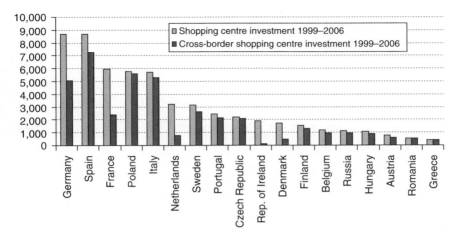

Figure 2.30 Investment in shopping centres, domestic and cross-border break-down, Europe, 1999–2006 (millions of euros)
Source: King Sturge(2008) *European Retail Property, Looking beyond the Benign*: 38.

Cross-border investment in shopping centres is also on the increase. In the period 1999–2004, cross-border purchases accounted for 68 per cent of total investment in shopping centres in Europe. In the cases of Poland, Greece, Czech Republic, Italy, Portugal and Finland, around 90 per cent of the capital invested in shopping centres came from outside the country. In the Netherlands, Denmark, France, Germany and the Republic of Ireland, by contrast, foreign capital accounted for less than 40 per cent of the total amount invested; see Figure 2.30. Cross-border investment amounted to 60 per cent of the total in 2006.

Yields

Since 2002, shopping centre yields have reduced continuously, particularly in Central and Eastern European countries such as Poland, with 5.25 per cent, or the Czech Republic with 5 per cent (King Sturge (2008) *European Retail Property, Looking beyond the Benign*: 3). The most mature markets in Western Europe, such as the United Kingdom, France, Italy and Switzerland, were also affected, with yields of between 4 per cent and 5 per cent. Indeed, the United Kingdom showed one of the lowest yields in Europe.

Industrial properties

The evolution of the industrial and logistic sector in Europe has followed a similar path to the other sectors: abundant liquidity in the

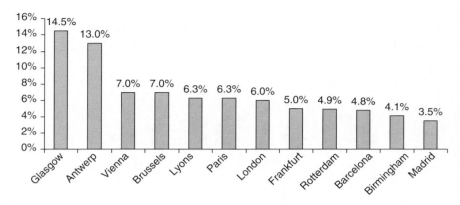

Figure 2.31   Vacancy rates of industrial property, Western Europe, Winter, 2005–6
Source: King Sturge (2006) *European Industrial Property Markets*: 3.

financial markets has had an impact on both prices and profit; increasing economic integration has driven business towards Europe, where awakening demand has influenced rents and yields; and the maintenance of acceptable GDP growth levels has sustained the continuous activity in this sector.

The industrial and logistic markets are influenced by the economic activity in each geographical area as well as by the adjacent areas, in particular with regard to production and international commerce.

Industrial space available

The city with the greatest industrial availability is Glasgow, in Scotland, followed by Antwerp in Belgium and Vienna in Austria, as can be seen from Figure 2.31. Within each city, vacancy rates tend to be lower in the city centre areas, where supply is more limited, since many industrial properties there are being converted to residential, retail, office or leisure use.

Evolution of industrial space

The supply of industrial space has increased unevenly across Europe. Part of the increase is related to pre-lease agreements with occupiers. Construction activity is strong in the Midlands and North of England (Birmingham and Manchester), the South of France

(Marseilles), Spain (Madrid and Valencia) and Poland (Warsaw), and to a lesser extent in the Czech Republic (Prague) and Romania (Bucharest). The Spanish market has maintained a fairly high level of new industrial installations in recent years, and in 2006 added 100,000 m² of logistical infrastructure (King Sturge (2007) *European Industrial Property Markets*: 1). In Western Europe, many old manufacturing plants have been removed because they no longer meet modern requirements.

In Central Europe, with the aim of satisfying the growth in demand for rentals, in 2006 and 2007 numerous projects were begun; most were in the Czech Republic (700,000 m²) and Poland (560,000 m²) (King Sturge (2007) *European Industrial Property Markets*: 1)

Rental market: demand

Demand in the warehouse segment is particularly high in Central Europe, northern France and Spain. Demand for other industrial buildings remains strong in the United Kingdom, Spain, Greece and Luxembourg. In 2006, rental demand increased as it was predicted by the economic recovery, and returned to the take-up levels of 2005. In France, new emergent areas such as Bordeaux have exceeded the demand in more consolidated areas such as Lyons (the take-up in these cities increased by 43 per cent and 13 per cent, respectively, in 2006 over 2005).

In Central and Eastern Europe, 2006 was a positive year for the two principal countries, namely the Czech Republic and Poland, with the demand level exceeding that of 2005 by 50 per cent and 75 per cent, respectively. In contrast, in Hungary the level decreased in 2006; see Figure 2.32 for the take-up level in selected cities.

Rents

Industrial rents tend to vary less than those of other sectors. In 2006, despite growing demand, the increases in rental rates were uneven. Over a one-year period there was a significant dispersion in the rate of change in rents across Europe: the largest increases were in Barcelona (21 per cent), Madrid (14 per cent), Edinburgh (10 per cent), Birmingham and Manchester (each 6 per cent), and Luxembourg and Lyons (each 5 per cent); see Figure 2.33. By contrast, the biggest decreases in rents were in Prague (−16 per cent), Budapest (−9 per cent), Warsaw (−8 per cent), Munich and Glasgow (−6 per cent for each), and Milan, Brussels and Genoa (−5 per cent for each). In Amsterdam, Antwerp and Rome, rents were unchanged.

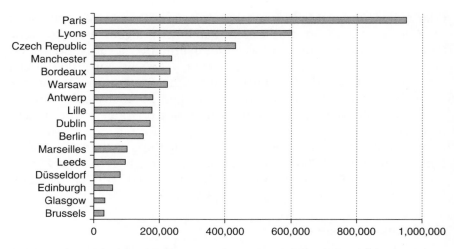

Figure 2.32   Take-up levels for selected European cities, 2006 (m²)
Note: Czech Republic represents all its cities, butPrague is the most active of them.
Source: King Sturge (2007) *European Industrial Property Markets*:18–56.

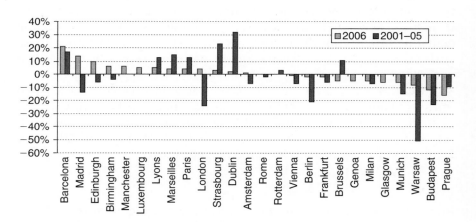

Figure 2.33   Variation in prime rents, selected European cities, over 1-year and
5-year periods, 2006 and 2001–5 (percentages)
Source: King Sturge (2006) (1Q) European *Industrial Property Markets*.

Over the five-year period 2001–5, we see a different picture. Dublin,
Genoa and Strasbourg had the biggest rent increases (32 per cent,
25 per cent and 23 per cent, respectively), while the greatest decreases
were in Warsaw, London and Budapest (−51 per cent, −24 per cent and
−23 per cent, respectively).

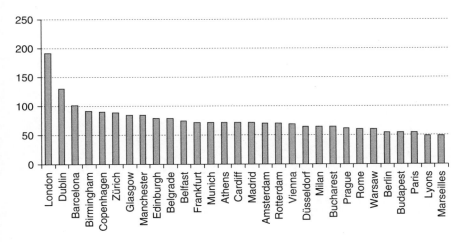

Figure 2.34 Industrial prime rents (properties of more than 5,000 m²), selected European cities, 2006 (euros/m²/year)
Source: King Sturge (2007) *European Industrial Property Markets*: 13.

Concerning prime rents of properties above 5,000 m², for the first quarter of 2006, London had the highest rent (190 euros per m² per year), followed by Dublin (120 euros per m² per year), and then Barcelona (96 euros per m² per year); see Figure 2.34.

Vacancy rate

The total available space in the Western European industrial sector decreased in 2006 (King Sturge, 2006 : 1) , apart from in the United Kingdom, where it grew, albeit only slightly. A similar tendency was observed in Central and Eastern Europe, where availability varied considerably from country to country. In Warsaw, for example, the industrial vacancy rate was 13 per cent, compared to 5 per cent in Budapest, and 3 per cent in Prague.

Investment market: volume

In 2004, 10 per cent of the total commercial real estate investment in the EU-15 went to the industrial sector. The bulk of this investment went to the United Kingdom, partly because it is one of Europe's largest markets but also because United Kingdom investors hold a particularly high proportion of their investments in industrial property. Both 2005 and 2006 saw sustained growth, even though a portion of the industrial market decreased because of low production rates.

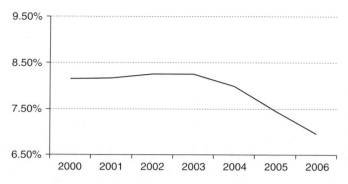

Figure 2.35 Industrial EU-15 yield index, 2000–6 (percentages)
Source: CB Richard Ellis (2006) *European Investment Market View*: 7.

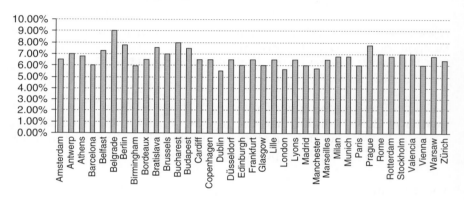

Figure 2.36 European prime industrial yields, 2006 (percentages)
Source: King Sturge (2007) *European Industrial Property Markets*: 15.

The cross-border nature of transport and distribution is intrinsic to the industrial sector and a prerequisite when analysing investment activity. The economic growth or decline of a region determines the distribution demand of adjacent areas.

Yield

In Western Europe, the markets have seen reductions in yields of up to 100 basis points, dropping to average levels of around 6.5 per cent; see Figure 2.35. This has led the players to look increasingly to international sources for new investment opportunities.

The compression of yields has occurred throughout Europe, including countries in Central and Eastern Europe, amid growing levels of investment. In Poland, for example, almost 200 million euros were invested in industrial real estate in 2006, 33 per cent more than in the previous year.

In general, the differences in yields across the European markets have continued to reduce, and in 2006 the difference between the principal European markets was less than 150 basis points (King Sturge (2007) *European Industrial Property Markets*: 14); see Figure 2.36.

Bibliography

Atisreal (2005–06) *European Office Market in Perspective.*
Atisreal (2006) *Europe Quarterly Office Markets* (Q4).
Atisreal (2007) *European Office Markets.*
CB Richard Ellis (2007) *Central London Offices* (Q4).
CB Richard Ellis (2006) *European Investment Market View.*
CB Richard Ellis (2006) *EU Shopping Centre Investment.*
Cushman and Wakefield (2006) *European Pipeline for 2006/2007* (April).
Cushman and Wakefield (2007) *European Shopping Centres.*
International Council of Shopping Centers (ICSC) (2005) *Towards a Pan-European Shopping Centre Standard – A Framework for International Comparison* (New York: ICSC).
Jones Lang LaSalle (2006) *European Office Property Clock* (4Q).
Jones Lang LaSalle (2006) *Shopping Centre Development Goes from Strength to Strength.*
Jones Lang LaSalle (2006, 2007) *European Capital Markets Bulletin.*
Jones Lang LaSalle (2006/07) *Office Supply Pipeline in Europe.*
Jones Lang LaSalle (2007) *Shopping Centre Development – The Boom Goes On.*
Jones Lang LaSalle (2007) *Central London Market Report* (Q4).
Jones Lang LaSalle (2007) *Key Market Indicators* (4Q).
Jones Lang LaSalle (2007) *Office Leasing Market Conditions in Europe* (March).
King Sturge (2005, 2006, 2007) *European Office Property Markets.*
King Sturge (2006, 2007) *European Industrial Property Markets* (2006, 2007).
King Sturge (2008) *European Retail Property, Looking Beyond the Benign.*
Knight Frank (2007) *European Investment Commentary* (Summer).
Lambert, J. (2006) 'One Step Closer to a Pan-European Shopping Center Standard', *ICSC Research Review*,13(2) (2006).
RREEF (2007) *The Future Size of the Global Real Estate Market* (July).

Market analysis company websites

www.atisreal.com
www.cbre.com
www.cushwake.com
www.joneslanglasalle.eu
www.kingsturge.com
www.knightfrank.com
www.rreef.com

3
Direct Property Investment

Since the mid-1990s, investment volume and prices in the European real estate markets have grown significantly. The industry's positive returns and low correlation with equity and fixed income investment, combined with greater market accessibility, have encouraged many investors to increase the weight of real estate assets in their investment portfolios, in an attempt to strike a more comfortable balance between risk and return.

One factor fuelling property investment was falling equity returns between 1999 and early 2003, prompting many investors to turn to real estate assets in search of higher returns. Between 1997 and 2006, the average annual return on an investment in the UK FTSE All Shares Index was 6.1 per cent, while direct property investment returned 13.6 per cent over the same period.

In addition to that, in recent years there has been an ample dissemination of information about real estate transactions that have boosted the confidence of investors and enhanced transparency. This information took the form of investment and rental reports from brokers, asset managers and business associations, and was further helped by the creation of property benchmarks.

In this chapter, I present the risk/return profile of investing in real estate. In Chapter 2 the yields from investing in commercial real estate were indicated for different asset classes and different locations. The yield is the upfront rate of return – that is, the return the property promises at the time of its purchase. If an investor buys the asset and holds it for a time, he or she would have a realized rate of return. This is the return discussed in this chapter, the actual rate of return of holding real estate investment in Europe. In order to perform a useful analysis of the data, some historical series are needed, which reduces the number of countries eligible. Consequently, in most of the chapter, only certain Western European countries are considered.

The final section is devoted to property derivatives. These are not properly direct investment in real estate but in fact they replicate such direct investment. Investors can take positions in real estate or hedge current positions by entering into derivatives contracts. These products have active markets in both the United Kingdom and the USA, but transactions have also been announced in other countries.

Characteristics of direct property investment

One distinctive characteristic of real estate investment is its low liquidity; property is not a readily marketable asset, unlike equities or bonds. On the other hand, real estate returns are much less changeable than equity returns: property is a less volatile asset. From 1976 to 2006, the FTSE Index had a volatility of 14.7 per cent (measured by the standard deviation of annual return) and the volatility of property investment in the United Kingdom was a much lower 8.7 per cent. Those volatilities were calculated from the data represented in Figure 3.1.

It could be argued that the high volatility of equity investments is the price that has to be paid for greater liquidity; the volatility of any

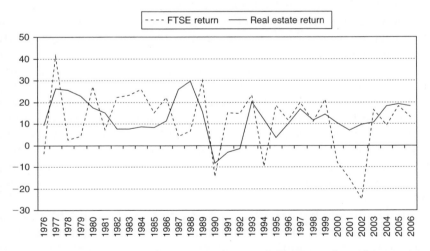

Figure 3.1　Return on investment in real estate (all property), and in equities, United Kingdom, 1976–2006 (annual percentage return, UK FTSE and IPD UK Property indices)

Sources: Investment Property Databank (IPD) and Thomson DataStream (both accessed June 2008).

asset is lower if the asset is valued infrequently. This may be one reason why equity investment is more volatile than direct property investment: equities are valued daily and are much more transparent, whereas property is valued much less frequently and less accurately, given the large number of private transactions taking place every day. Although this may influence the calculation of an asset's volatility, equity investment is still far more volatile than direct property investment.

One consequence of real estate investment is the management burden required for property operation and the ordinary expenses arising from the rental, maintenance or conservation of properties. Frequently an investor in real estate has to hire more than one specialist in order to accomplish the tasks required for the preservation of an asset.

Direct real estate investment carries high transaction costs, both for the buyer and for the seller, as well as high administrative and management costs. In addition to different taxes, the change in ownership normally implies legal and brokerage expenses (Chapter 1 includes the cost of purchasing houses in different European countries).

Another characteristic is that real estate assets are heterogeneous – they are not fungible or interchangeable. Traditionally, it has been said that the three rules of real estate business are 'location, location, location'; but in spite of this, the current sophistication of the industry has demonstrated that real estate activity comprises much more than location.

Real estate investment offers excellent opportunities to take advantage of financial leverage as a result of its income-generating capacity and the lower volatility of prices. This permits investors to leverage returns more frequently and more heavily than in other asset classes. This is an advantage compared to other assets that have to be financed with a higher proportion of equity.

The benefits of using debt are enhanced by the tax-deductibility of interest paid on loans. Another tax advantage is that the value of a property is depreciated each year to account for obsolescence or deterioration. This decrease in value may also be recorded as a tax-deductible expense. Obviously, this will increase the investor's taxable profit on disposal of the property, but it has a favourable impact on time-adjusted rates of return.

Some of these characteristics of real estate assets (they are difficult to standardize; they have highly localized markets; large numbers of confidential transactions are conducted daily; infrequent trading, for example) leads to much of the data coming from private sources and those data are, as a result, fragmented, expensive and elusive.

It has often been said in recent years that the real estate market has high capitalization potential, in the sense that many real estate assets eventually gain a stock market listing. It has been estimated that only 4 per cent of the institutional-grade real estate assets in the whole of Europe (excluding the United Kingdom) was held by listed property companies (Bigman and Chiu, 2005). Moreover, REITs (real estate investment trusts) are now being introduced in the main European countries (see Chapter 4).

Real estate investment benchmarks and indices

Since 2003, and despite the fact that most industry transactions are private, some organizations have developed property benchmarks and indices for different European markets, contributing to transparency, confidence, and eventually to an increase in investment, whether domestic, international or inter-regional. As it is complicated to construct benchmarks using actual transaction prices, appraisal values are used instead. This might smooth the flow of returns, perhaps giving a more than appropriate impression of stability.

One of the oldest of the well-known benchmarks is UK-based Investment Property Databank (IPD), created in 1971. IPD covers twenty-three countries, most of them in Europe, although Australia, Canada, South Africa, Japan, Korea and New Zealand are also included. Since 2001, IPD has published a pan-European index, subsequently followed by other aggregate indices: a Central and Eastern Europe index, a Nordic index and a Global index. Table 3.1 displays information from IPD's country indices.

There are also benchmarks from sources in others countries, such as NCREIF (National Council of Real Estate Investment Fiduciaries) in the USA, and from official departments in Australia and New Zealand. In general, when using these benchmarks in different studies it is necessary to understand how they are calculated (for example, the category of assets covered; if all the sources of profitability are included; what values are considered) in order to ensure direct comparability. These indices of property returns have greatly enhanced market transparency.

Risk–return profile of direct property investment, all-property

Total risk and return

Total return of property investment is the sum of capital growth (the increase in value) and income return (that coming from rents). The main segments of real estate and those analysed in this chapter are

Table 3.1   Benchmarks in the European direct real estate market, as at end 2006

	Index started	No. of properties	Total capital value covered (millions of euros)	Investment market size (millions of euros)	Percentage of each market (est.)
Austria	2004	908	7,798	21,934	36
Belgium	2005	200	4,400	n.a.	n.a.
Denmark	2000	1,222	12,056	29,771	40
Finland	1998	2,830	17,116	27,935	61
France	1986	7,518	99,558	159,888	62
Germany	1996	2,938	53,847	251,268	21
Republic of Ireland	1984	331	5,820	7,064	82
Italy	2003	840	13,763	57,774	24
Netherlands	1995	5,369	45,174	72,525	62
Norway	2000	497	10,817	24,412	44
Portugal	2000	587	7,795	14,617	53
Spain	2001	549	15,569	29,337	53
Sweden	1984	1,027	21,880	64,308	34
Switzerland	2002	3,478	29,350	78,135	38
United Kingdom	1971	12,137	284,662	520,823	55
All IPD Europe		**40,431**	**629,605**	**1,359,791**	**46**

Source: Investment Property Databank (IPD) (accessed June 2008).

residential, office, retail and industrial. This paragraph is devoted to all these segments taken together, what is called 'all-property'.

In general, there have been good returns in property investment in most countries. There are many returns at or above the 10 per cent level, all of them being direct, non-leveraged returns. Most returns exceed the inflation rate, though Germany is an exception here; see Table 3.2.

The United Kingdom offered the highest 3-year return. For the UK, the shorter the selected period, the higher the return. As can be seen in Figure 3.2, while there is a return of 18.5 per cent for the 3-year period, it is just 13.5 per cent for the 10-year period. With regard to profitability over the 3-year period, in second and third place are Spain and Norway, with returns of 15.3 per cent and 14.4 per cent, respectively.

France and Sweden are in fourth and fifth places in the 3-year rate of return, respectively, with 14.0 per cent and 11.5 per cent. In Sweden, the rate of return at 8 and 10 years is better than at 5 years because of

Table 3.2 Annual totals, all-property returns and inflation, selected European countries, 1995–2006 (nominal, in local currency; percentages)

	1995	1996	1997	1998	1999	2000	2001	2002	2003	2004	2005	2006
Annual total returns												
Germany		4.7	3.5	4	4.9	5.4	5.6	4.1	3.2	1.3	0.5	1.3
Denmark						10.2	11.4	9.4	7.3	6.3	10.2	15.4
Spain							9.1	8.2	8.3	11.5	17.2	17.4
France				3.6	13.4	15.2	9.7	8.6	8.1	10.1	12.6	21.8
Netherlands	10.7	11.7	12.6	13.6	15.7	16	11.4	8.8	7.1	7.7	10.2	12.5
Norway						12.8	10.8	7	7.6	10.4	15.2	17.6
Portugal						10.8	13.1	13.8	10	10.6	10.5	12
United Kingdom	3.6	10	16.8	11.8	14.5	10.5	6.8	9.6	10.9	18.3	19.1	18.1
Sweden			10.7	14.4	17.5	21.9	4.6	2.4	0.9	5.8	12.7	16.2
Switzerland								5.7	5.1	4.9	5.2	5.9
Inflation												
Germany	1.7	1.5	1.9	0.9	0.6	1.5	2.0	1.4	1.1	1.7	2.0	1.7
Denmark						2.9	2.4	2.4	2.1	1.2	1.8	1.9
Spain							3.6	3.1	3.0	3.0	3.4	3.5
France				0.6	0.5	1.7	1.6	1.9	2.1	2.1	1.7	1.7
Netherlands	1.9	2	2.2	2	2.2	2.4	4.2	3.3	2.1	1.2	1.7	1.4
Norway						3.1	3.0	1.3	2.5	0.5	1.5	2.3
Portugal						2.9	4.3	3.6	3.3	2.4	2.3	3.1
United Kingdom	3.4	2.5	3.1	3.4	1.6	2.9	1.8	1.6	2.9	3.0	2.8	3.2
Sweden			0.5	-0.1	0.4	1.0	2.4	2.1	1.9	0.3	0.4	1.4
Switzerland								0.6	0.6	0.8	1.2	1.1

Sources: Investment Property Databank (IPD), Thomson DataStream (both accessed June 2008).

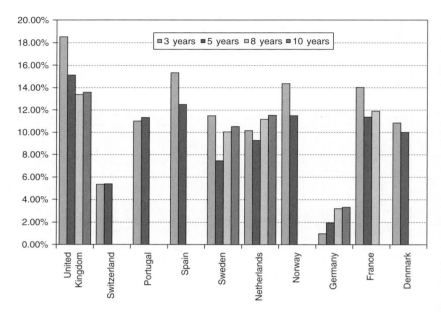

Figure 3.2 Total nominal all-property returns, selected European countries, 1997–2006 (in local currencies; percentages)
Note: The 10-year annual return is the geometric mean of the returns from 1995 to 2004; the 8-year return, from 1999 to 2006; the 5-year return, from 2002 to 2006; and the 3-year return, from 2004 to 2006.
Source: Investment Property Databank (IPD) (accessed June 2008).

the annual decrease between 2001 and 2004. In France, the 8-year rate of return is higher than the 5-year rate, because of the fall from 8.3 per cent to 6.7 per cent in 2002.

Portugal and Denmark are in sixth and seventh place when considering average returns for the 3-year period, with 11 per cent and 10.8 per cent, respectively. In Portugal, the 8-year rate of return is marginally better than the 5-year rate, because of the slightly decreasing trend in the rate of return between 2002 and 2004. In Denmark, the 3-year rate of return is better than the 5-year rate. This is because of the slight tendency towards a decrease in the 2002 to 2004 annual rates of return, going from 10.4 per cent to 7 per cent. This was recouped in 2005 with a rate of 10.2 per cent.

In last place was Germany, with a 3-year rate of return of 1 per cent. The German real estate industry showed very low returns for all timeframes.

As it is the case with most investment, the real rate of return is a relevant measure. Real returns are calculated by subtracting the inflation

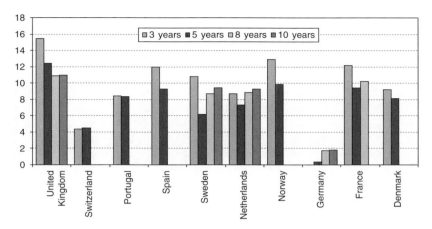

Figure 3.3 Total real all-property returns, selected European countries, 1997–2006 (local currencies; percentages)
Source: Investment Property Databank (IPD) (accessed June 2008).

rate from the nominal return. The United Kingdom again offers the best 3-year return (15.5 per cent), but also has a larger return when the real rate of return on all properties is measured for periods of 5, 8 and 10 years in length; see Figure 3.3.

In the 3-year range, the second most profitable country is Norway, with a real return of 12.9 per cent. In third place is France (12.2 per cent), followed by Spain (12 per cent), Sweden (10.8 per cent), Denmark (9.2 per cent), the Netherlands (8.7 per cent) and Switzerland (4.5 per cent). These countries all follow the same pattern as in the nominal return. The last place is for Germany, the only country with a negative return (−0.8 per cent).

The risk of an investment is usually represented by its variability measured by the standard deviation of its returns. The standard deviation of the returns was calculated for those countries with data available from 2000 to 2006, so as to reflect the variability over seven years; see Figure 3.4.

The greatest variability of return is found in Sweden, well above the others, followed by France and the United Kingdom, which have very similar values and form a category of their own. Norway, the Netherlands, Denmark, Germany and Portugal are placed in order of decreasing value, with the last two countries having very low volatility.

The risk-and-return trade-off is shown in Figure 3.5 for the period 2000–06. There are eight countries with the required data; the United Kingdom appears twice, with data for thirty-six years (shown in

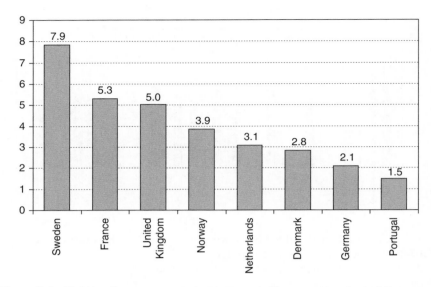

Figure 3.4   Risk in direct property investment, all-property, selected European countries, 2000–6 (standard deviation of annual returns; percentages)
Source: Investment Property Databank (IPD) (accessed June 2008).

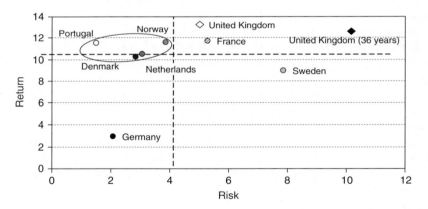

Figure 3.5   Nominal real estate risks and returns, all property, selected European countries, 2000–6 (in local currencies; percentages)
Source: Investment Property Databank (IPD) (accessed June 2008).

brackets). The return is the geometric mean of the annual returns for the period 2000–6, while the risk is the typical deviation of the annual returns for the same period. The dotted lines are the average risk and return of the countries studied. The normal quadrants are the upper

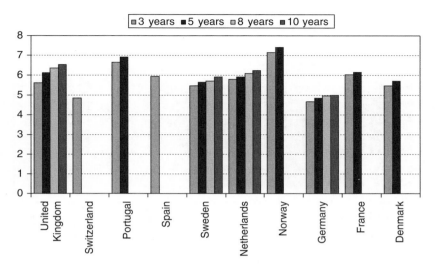

Figure 3.6 Nominal annual income returns, selected European countries, 1997–2006 (local currencies; percentages)
Source: Investment Property Databank (IPD) (accessed June 2008).

right and the bottom left ones, with superior risk and return, or lower risk and return than average measures.

The three countries with above-average return and below-average risk are Portugal, Norway and the Netherlands, in the upper-left quadrant, Denmark is just in the average return, with below-average risk. These four countries offer a similar average rate of return for the period studied, of around 11.5 per cent. The best combination could be identified in Portugal, which shows the lowest risk and almost the same return as Norway. Sweden is the only country in the lower-right quadrant, which is the most unfavourable combination; it exhibits a lower-than-average return and a higher-than-average risk.

As noted earlier, total return is the result of income return plus capital growth. Income return is supposed to be more stable over time because it comes from the renting of properties. This stability gives real estate investment more debt capacity and allows for higher multiples when valuing cash flows.

The stable pattern of annual income returns is evident from Figure 3.6. Even though the variations are limited, overall, income return decreased over the period 1997–2006; in most of the countries the annual return decreases as the period taken for the calculation is reduced. The countries offering the highest 3-year income return are Norway (7.1 per cent), Portugal (6.6 per cent) and France (6.0 per cent).

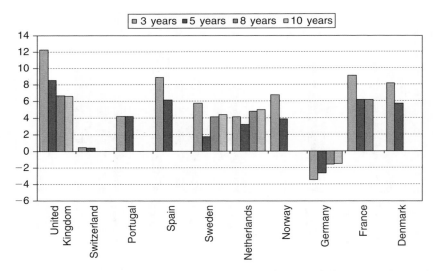

Figure 3.7   Nominal capital growth when investing in all-properties, selected
European countries, 1997–2006 (local currencies; percentages)
Source: Investment Property Databank (IPD) (accessed June 2008).

Capital growth is more volatile. In general terms, it decreased over
the period 1997–2003 and grew significantly between 2004 and 2006,
which explains why, in the majority of the countries studied, 5-year
capital growth was less than that of 8-year growth. On the other hand,
3-year capital growth was greater than that of the 5-year period and, in
some cases, exceeded 8-year capital growth; see Figure 3.7. The improve-
ment of capital growth in the later years is related to the decrease in the
income return. The countries with the highest 3-year capital growth
are the United Kingdom (12.3 per cent), France (9.1 per cent) and Spain
(8.9 per cent).

Switzerland and Germany have the lowest 3-year income returns in
Europe, at around 5 per cent, as well as the lowest capital growth.
Switzerland had growth of 0.5 per cent, whereas Germany was placed
last, with negative 3-year growth of −3.5 per cent.

Sweden had a 3-year income return of 5.5 per cent and capital growth
of 5.7 per cent, compared to the 5-year rates of income return at 5.7 per
cent and capital growth at 1.7 per cent. Figure 3.7 reflects the sudden
reversal in the Swedish market, from a 15.6 per cent return in the year
2000 to −1 per cent, −3.4 per cent in 2002, −4.8 per cent in 2003 and
0 per cent in 2004. In 2005, the capital growth recovered to 7 per cent
and then grew to 10.5 per cent in 2006.

Norway offered the best 3-year income returns in Europe (7.2 per cent) and capital growth of 6.8 per cent. It also had the highest 5-year income return, contrasting with low 5-year capital growth, thanks to the lower capital growth rates between 2001 and 2003, with negative rates in 2002 and 2003. Portugal also delivered a high income return (6.6 per cent) and more modest capital growth of around 4 per cent for both the 3-year and the 5-year periods.

The Netherlands' 3-year income return was 5.8 per cent, although the return decreased slightly from the 10-year to the 3-year period, as shown in Figure 3.7. Meanwhile, capital growth increased from 1997 to 2000, when it reached 9 per cent, only to decline sharply in 2001, reaching 1.6 per cent in 2004 then recovering again with an annual capital growth of 4.2 per cent in 2005 and 6.6 per cent in 2006.

Finally, France and Denmark offered a 3-year income return of around 6 per cent. In France, the rental market grew steadily, but the investment market suffered an abrupt downturn in 2001, falling from 8 per cent to 1.6 per cent in 2003. In Denmark, 3-year capital growth was 8.1 per cent. As in France, the rate declined in 2003 (0.9 per cent) but later rose sharply to 11.9 per cent, and remained at that level in 2006.

Volatility of income returns and capital growth

To measure the volatility of returns, the risk imbedded in the series, the standard deviation of those returns were calculated where data for the most recent seven years exist – that is, 2000–6. As may be anticipated, capital growth is much more volatile than income returns. Property rents are normally fixed for an agreed period in lease contracts, whereas property values vary with supply and demand.

Figure 3.8 presents the standard deviation of income and capital growth. The volatility of each component of total return could be compare with the volatility of total return illustrated in Figure 3.4 for the same 7-year period, 2000–6. The standard deviation of income in the United Kingdom comes first (0.74), followed by Portugal (0.52), and Denmark (0.52). In joint last place are France (0.26) and the Netherlands (0.23).

The risk of capital growth does not follow the same order of volatility as in Figure 3.4. In the case of standard deviation of capital growth, Sweden is in first place, with high volatility (7.7 per cent), followed by the United Kingdom, France and Denmark, all with similar volatility but in a different order from that of Figure 3.4. Bringing up the rear are Germany (1.7 per cent) and Portugal, which has the lowest volatility in Europe (1.3 per cent).

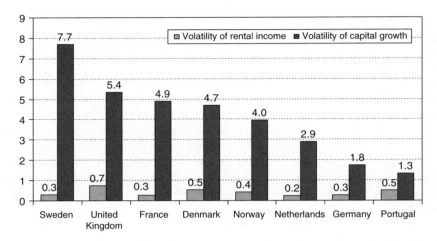

Figure 3.8   Volatility of rental income and capital growth, selected European countries, 2000–6 (standard deviation; percentages)
Source: Investment Property Databank (IPD) (accessed June 2008).

Risk and return on direct property investment by property asset class

The characteristics of the risk and return of investment in the different asset classes – residential, office, retail, and industrial – will be presented from the data for the most recent 7-year period for which data is available, covering the year 2000 to 2006.

Return of property investment by sector

In most countries, the sectors offering the highest returns are retail and residential; see Figure 3.9. No data are available for the residential market in the United Kingdom. In the United Kingdom and France, the industrial sector is in second place, behind retail.

The countries with the highest returns in retail property are France, with a 7-year annual return of 16.7 per cent, and Spain, with 14.3 per cent; behind them are the United Kingdom, Norway and Portugal, each with a 7-year annual return of between 13 per cent and 14 per cent.

There were exceptional rates of return in the *retail sector* in 2005. In France, this sector offered particularly high returns during that year, with an annual rate of return of 26.2 per cent, as can be seen from Figure 3.10. Spain also experienced high performance in 2005, with a return of 20.3 per cent.

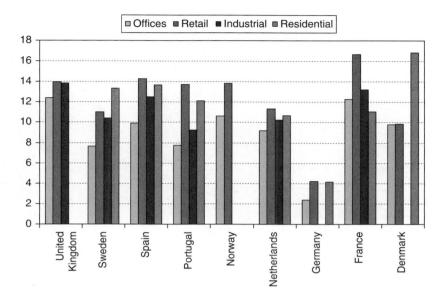

Figure 3.9 Total nominal 7-year property returns, selected European countries, 2000–6 (local currencies; percentages)
Source: Investment Property Databank (IPD) (accessed June 2008).

The United Kingdom had recorded very low annual returns in 2000 and 2001; in fact, the second-lowest of the countries studied, not rising above 6.5 per cent in either year. However, from 2002 onwards, it was always among the most profitable countries. In Norway, there was sustained growth in the retail sector annual return between 2000 and 2006. In Portugal, by contrast, there were no such sharp movements in the retail annual return between 2000 and 2006.

Continuing with the profitability of the retail sector, the Netherlands and Sweden follow Portugal, offering 7-year returns of 11.4 per cent and 11 per cent, respectively. In both countries the retail sector return increased. From 2004 onwards, there was a growth in returns in most countries. The Netherlands and Sweden were no exception to this, with returns ranging between 9 per cent and 10 per cent during the period 2000–4, with the former recording returns above 13 per cent in both 2005 and 2006. In the case of Sweden, the return grew from a range of 7–10 per cent during 2000–4 to rates above 17 per cent.

Next is Denmark, offering 7-year returns of 9.8 per cent. There was a slight deceleration in the Danish retail sector during 2003, when the return fell from 10.4 per cent to 7.1 per cent. This downward trend continued in 2004, but eventually recovered in 2005. Last of all

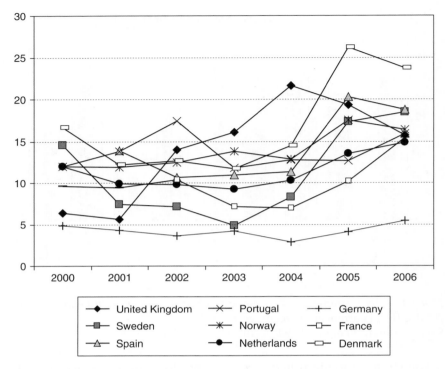

Figure 3.10   Total annual return, retail sector, selected European countries, 2000–6 (percentages)
Source: Investment Property Databank (IPD) (accessed June 2008).

was Germany, whose retail sector performed well below the European average, with a return of around 4.0 per cent over the 5-year period.

Turning to *residential property*, the country offering the highest 7-year annual return was Denmark, with 16.8 per cent (the highest in Europe in any sector over the 7-year period, as can be seen from Figure 3.11). Lower residential returns were observed in Spain, with 13.7 per cent, and Sweden, with 13.4 per cent. In Denmark, there was a very strong increase in the annual residential sector return in 2005, rising from 11.1 per cent in the previous year to reach 38.1 per cent. It fell again in 2006 but at the time of writing remains the highest in all the European sectors at 24.2 per cent.

In Spain and Sweden there were no such sharp changes in the annual residential sector return between 2000 and 2006, but certain trends can still be identified, albeit more subtle ones, in the historic values: low in Spain, reducing from 15 per cent in 2002 to 10.2 per cent in 2006; and

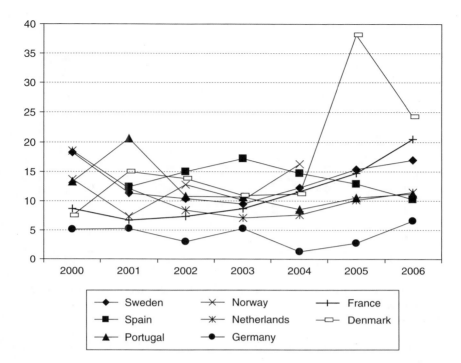

Figure 3.11 Total annual return, residential sector, selected European countries, 2000–6 (percentages)

Note: No data is available for Norway after 2004.

Source: Investment Property Databank (IPD) (accessed June 2008).

higher in Sweden (from 10.4 per cent in 2002 to 16.9 per cent in 2006). These countries were followed by Portugal, France and the Netherlands, offering 7-year returns of 12.1 per cent, 11 per cent and 10.7 per cent, respectively. In Portugal, the annual returns of the sector during the period studied were fairly stable at between 13 per cent and 11 per cent, registering only two sharp movements: an increase from 13 per cent in 2000 to 20.6 per cent in 2001, and a decrease in 2004 from 10.6 per cent to 8.5 per cent.

The Netherlands' residential sector delivered a sharp decrease in returns during 2002–4, falling from an annual return of 18.5 per cent in 2000 to rates of between 8.4 per cent and 7.6 per cent, but rebounded in 2005 and 2006, to 10.1 per cent and 11 per cent, respectively. France has experienced sustained growth from 2001 to the time of writing, with returns increasing from 6.7 per cent to 20.5 per cent in 2006. In last place was Germany, having a 7-year return of 4.2 per cent, below

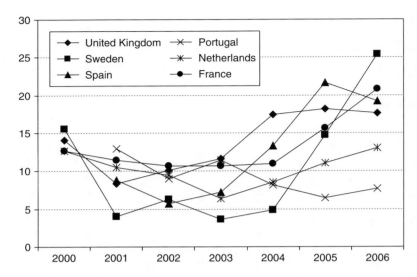

Figure 3.12   Total annual return, industrial sector, selected European countries, 2000–6 (percentages)
Source: Investment Property Databank (IPD) (accessed June 2008).

the European average, with 2004 seeing a sharp fall from 5.3 per cent to 1.3 per cent.

The countries with the highest returns in the *industrial sector* are the United Kingdom, with a 7-year return of 13.8 per cent, France with 13.2 per cent, and Spain with 12.5 per cent. The United Kingdom's returns grew from 8.3 per cent in 2001 to between 17.5 per cent and 18.2 per cent in 2004–6. In France, there were signs of similar movements, but it was not until 2005 that the rate increased substantially, from 11 per cent to 15.7 per cent, and ended 2006 at 20.8 per cent. Spain followed a similar trend, observing maximum values in 2005 of 21.7 per cent, but still attracted attention because this was the country that, in 2002, had the smallest annual return in the European sector (5.7 per cent), but in 2005 became the country with the highest; see Figure 3.12.

In fourth place was Sweden, with a 7-year return of 10.4 per cent. The Swedish industrial sector, as with the Spanish one, went from being one of the lowest in Europe to one of the highest. In 2003 and 2004, the return was 3.7 per cent and 6.3 per cent, the lowest in Europe in those years, followed by very strong growth in 2005 resulting in the highest 2006 return in Europe for the period (25.4 per cent).

In fifth place was the Netherlands, with a 7-year return of 10.2 per cent. Between 2000 and 2003, the sector's return fell steadily from 12.7 per cent to finally reach 6.4 per cent, but recovered in the following

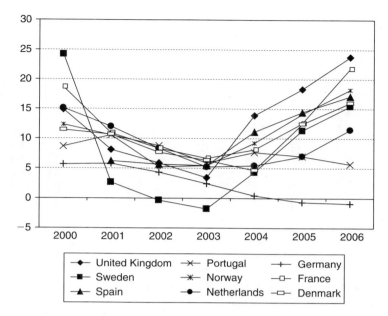

Figure 3.13 Total annual return, office sector, selected European countries, 2000–6 (percentages)
Source: Investment Property Databank (IPD) (accessed June 2008).

three years to reach 13 per cent in 2006. In last place is Portugal, with a 7-year return of 9.3 per cent; its profitability dropped from 11.4 per cent in 2003 to 7.7 per cent in 2006.

The *office sector* had the lowest returns in the European property market, following a deep recession in this sector between 2000 and 2003. The rate of return on office property declined steeply from 2001, because of slack European economic growth. It recovered in most countries in 2004, however; see Figure 3.13. The correlation between returns and the general economy is observed in all sectors, but is more evident in the industrial and office sectors.

Office sector returns are led by the United Kingdom, with a 7-year average of 12.4 per cent, France with 12.3 per cent and Norway with 10.6 per cent. As a general rule, the trend followed by the sector has been the same in all countries. Starting from high returns in 2000, compared with those recorded in subsequent years, they fell sharply from 2001 as a result of the world recession, and bottomed out in 2003. After 2004, their performance began to recover, attaining rates in 2006 that were equal to or above those obtained before the recession. The only countries that did not follow this trend were Portugal and Germany.

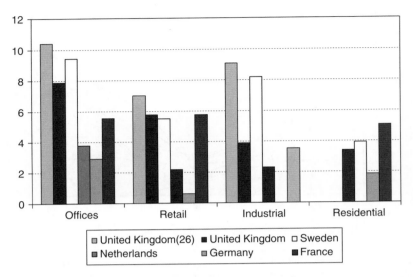

Figure 3.14   Investment risk by asset class, five European countries, 2000–6*
(standard deviation of returns; percentages)
Note: *United Kingdom(26) is United Kingdom dataset over a 26-year period.
Source: Investment Property Databank (IPD) (accessed June 2008).

These countries were not able to recover after the recession and the sector's performance continued to fall there.

Sweden saw the biggest drop in this sector in Europe in 2001, from 24.2 per cent to 2.7 per cent, reaching a low of −1.8 per cent in 2003. The Swedish real estate industry experienced a brief recession, not only in office property but also in the residential, retail and industrial sectors, as shown previously. Last of all was Germany, where the rate of return on office property fell from 5.7 per cent in 2000 to −0.9 per cent in 2006, with the 7-year return a mere 2.4 per cent.

Risk of investment in different asset classes

As a proxy for the risk incurred in investment in different asset classes, the standard deviation of returns were calculated for countries with the required data. This is illustrated in Figure 3.14, which includes data for five countries, plus a second dataset for the United Kingdom over a 26-year period to highlight the behaviour of risk in longer time spans. The following comments do not take into account the values for the 26-year period in the United Kingdom.

The office sector in Sweden had the highest variability (9.4 per cent); and it was also the highest variability of any sector. Sweden is followed closely by the United Kingdom (7.9 per cent), France (5.8 per cent) and the Netherlands (3.8 per cent). In last place is Germany (2.9 per cent). The country ranking in the office sector is close to that of Figure 3.4.

In the retail sector, France had the highest volatility (5.9 per cent), followed by the United Kingdom (5.8 per cent) and Sweden (5.5 per cent). The Netherlands and Germany, by contrast, have low volatility (at 2.2 per cent and 0.6 per cent, respectively).

In the industrial sector, Sweden once again had the highest risk (8.19 per cent). Far behind Sweden's values, in second and third place, were the United Kingdom and France, with 3.88 per cent and 3.75 per cent, respectively. The United Kingdom and France not only had the highest 5-year return in the industrial sector, but also the lowest volatility in Europe (2.5 per cent).

Residential sector volatility was highest in France (4.9 per cent), followed by the Netherlands (3.9 per cent) and very closely by Sweden (3.4 per cent). As in the other sectors, the country with the lowest volatility in residential property was Germany (1.8 per cent). In general, residential volatility was lower than that in the other asset classes.

Risk and return profile

The historical combination of risk and return for all studied countries and asset classes could shed some light on the characteristics of the investment in each one, at least in very recent times. Geometric mean of annual returns and standard deviation for 2000–06 are depicted in Figure 3.15. Two lines were drawn, for average return and average volatility.

In the upper-left quadrant are the countries and sectors with returns above the European average, and with below-average risk. Retail sector investment predominates in this quadrant, and the sector/country with the highest return here is retail/Spain. The second highest return is for the United Kingdom's industrial sector. Following closely in terms of profitability are Norway and Portugal, again, in the retail sector, and Spanish residential sector, which offer a lower return than the United Kingdom, but also less risk. Spanish residential investment had record house price growth between 2000 and 2006.

The upper-right quadrant comprises the countries and sectors with above-average return and above-average risk. The points with the highest return are residential investment in Denmark, which has the highest risk of all, followed by retail sector investment in France. The next highest are retail sector investment in the United Kingdom, followed by the Spanish industrial sector and the French and United Kingdom office sectors, which offer similar returns but with different measures of risk.

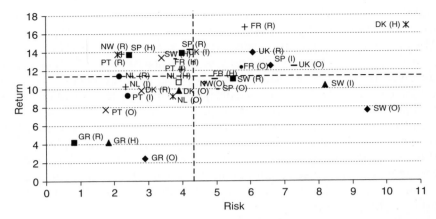

Figure 3.15 Risk and return of property investment, by sector, European countries, 2000–6 (geometric mean of annual returns and standard deviation; percentages)

Note: (R) retail; (H) residential; (I) industrial; (O) office; (DK) Denmark; (FR) France; (GR) Germany; (NL) Netherlands; (NW) Norway; (PT) Portugal; (SP) Spain; (SW) Sweden; (UK) United Kingdom.
Source: Investment Property Databank (IPD) (accessed June 2008).

The lower quadrants are dominated by the office sector. On the left are all the German property sectors, while, in the lower-right quadrant and contrasting with the situation in most European countries, is retail sector investment in Sweden, with below-average returns and above-average risk. The industrial sector is scattered across all four quadrants.

International diversification across Europe

From an investor's point of view, given the highly local nature of the real estate markets, in general, low correlation coefficients are found and, consequently, international diversification often enhances a portfolio's risk/return trade-off. This is one of the factors behind the increased proportion of cross-border investment within total direct real estate investment (see Chapter 2).

Even more importantly in Europe, economic integration and the adoption of the euro has greatly assisted the establishment of an international operations network, thus stimulating intra-regional investment. Cross-border investment predominated in many European countries, accounting for 83 per cent of total investment in France in 2007, 52 per cent in the United Kingdom, and 46 per cent in Germany (this country down from 71 per cent in 2006). On the other hand, in smaller, more mature national markets, domestic investment predominated, as was

Table 3.3 Correlation of annual returns on direct property investment, selected European countries, 1997–2006

	United Kingdom	Sweden	Netherlands	Germany	France
United Kingdom	1	0.2928	−0.0544	−0.8106	0.4111
Sweden		1	0.8856	0.1391	0.5746
Netherlands			1	0.5408	0.4200
Germany				1	−0.1807
France					1

Source: Investment Property Databank (IPD) (accessed June 2008).

the case in Norway (97 per cent of domestic investment in 2007), the Republic of Ireland (94 per cent), and Portugal (76 per cent).

The low correlation among different European real estate national markets means that investors can improve the risk/return combination of their portfolios through international diversification. Table 3.3 shows the correlation between direct property investment returns in different European countries. As can be seen from the Table, only the Netherlands and Sweden had a significant coefficient during this period.

Analysis can be conducted for Western European countries as they have larger volumes of transactions and a longer series of historical data available. Until recent years, only a relatively small amount of total investment has been directed towards Central and Eastern Europe, but at the time of writing the percentage of funds going to this region is increasing faster than the total. Many countries have joined the EU recently and many of them subsequently (and perhaps as a consequence) experienced rapid growth. The property markets of Central Europe are becoming increasingly sophisticated and in many respects more comparable to those in Western European countries; at the time of writing (see Table 3.4).

Greater political stability, stable legal frameworks and the preparation for the adoption of the euro has also fuelled interest in commercial real estate. The biggest individual transactions in Hungary, Poland and the Czech Republic have been in the retail (shopping centres) sector. Housing is one of the most promising sectors, because of the need to restore existing stock, and the prospective growth of main cities and the increased availability of mortgages – even though the population is decreasing in some of these countries. The logistics, distribution and industrial sectors have also become more popular as these countries' economies develop, and there is a similar situation with offices. Other

Table 3.4   Countries with recent EU accession

Country	Population (millions)	GDP (millions euros)	GDP per capita (euros)	Accession date
Cyprus	0.8	14,522	18,958	May 2004
Slovakia	5.4	43,945	8,138	May 2004
Slovenia	2.0	29,742	14,871	May 2004
Estonia	1.4	13,074	9,339	May 2004
Hungary	10.1	89,884	8,899	May 2004
Latvia	2.3	16,180	7,035	May 2004
Lithuania	3.5	23,746	6,785	May 2004
Malta	0.4	5,096	12,740	May 2004
Poland	38.6	271,530	7,034	May 2004
Czech Republic	10.3	113,969	11,065	May 2004
Bulgaria	7.8	25,100	3,218	January 2007
Romania	22.3	97,118	4,355	January 2007
EU-15	389.5	10,817,799	27,774	
EU-27	493.0	11,561,706	23,453	

Source: European Mortgage Federation (2007) *Hypostat 2006* (November).

important sectors are hotels and resorts, as many of these countries are becoming tourist destinations.

Total real estate returns and macroeconomic variables

Correlation of real estate returns (all-property) with interest rates and GDP

The available data about interest rates and real estate returns in the all-property index is depicted in Figure 3.16. In the period 2001–06 a positive correlation is evident: from 2001 to 2003 both variables decline, and then both increase in the rest of the period. It is apparent that a longer period of time is needed before it is possible to comment more deeply on the relationship between these variables.

As it is hypothesized, a relationship exists between general economic activity and real estate performance, and in particular a positive relationship is expected between the demand for offices and industrial properties with the change in GDP. The increased demand for assets could prompt both prices and returns to rise. This relationship is explored in Figure 3.17. Data for the United Kingdom, France, Germany, the Netherlands, Sweden, Spain, Portugal, Denmark and Norway are included for the purposes of calculating the aggregate return on direct

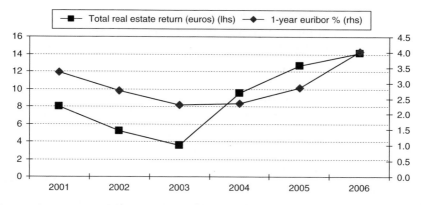

Figure 3.16   Real estate return and interest rates, Europe, 2001–6 (percentages)
Note: Total real estate return measured by the Pan-European Property Index (IPD). Euribor is the European interbank offered rate.
Sources: Investment Property Databank (IPD), European Mortgage Federation, Thomson DataStream (all accessed June 2008).

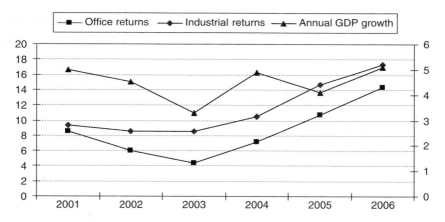

Figure 3.17   Returns on direct investment in office and industrial property (lhs), and annual GDP growth (rhs), EU-15, 2001–6 (percentages)
Sources: OECD, European Central Bank, Investment Property Databank (IPD), Thomson DataStream (all accessed June 2008).

investment in offices and industrial property. The annual GDP growth is that of EU-15.

The slight relationship apparent in Figure 3.17 is measured more precisely in Table 3.5, which presents the correlation coefficient between total annual returns of office and industrial sectors, on the one hand, and GDP annual growth, on the other.

Table 3.5   Correlation between GDP growth and direct investment returns on office and industrial property, EU-15, 2001–6

	GDP growth
Office returns	0.63
Industrial returns	0.51

Sources: OECD, European Central Bank, Investment Property Databank (IPD), Thomson DataStream (both accessed June 2008).

Direct real estate investment versus equities and bonds

In order to show the performance of real estate investments *vis-à-vis* equities and bonds, data from the United Kingdom is used because of the availability of longer historical series for that country. In the United Kingdom during the period 1978–2006, the most profitable investment was in real estate. In second place was investment in equities, a position to which it returned after the decline in its index between 1999 and 2002. The least profitable investment was in bonds but, nevertheless, all three indices beat inflation; see Figure 3.18.

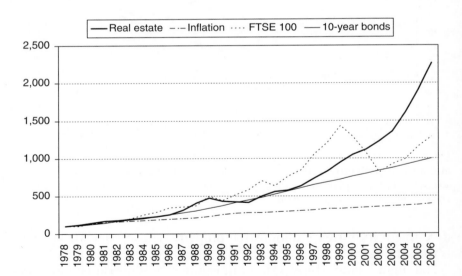

Figure 3.18   Cumulative returns on direct investment in real estate and other asset classes, United Kingdom, 1978–2006 (December 1978 = 100)
Sources: Investment Property Databank (IPD), Thomson DataStream (both accessed June 2008).

Table 3.6 Annual average returns and standard deviations of real estate, equities and bonds, United Kingdom, 1979–2006

	United Kingdom	
	Returns (%)	Standard deviation (%)
Direct real estate investment	11.8	8.4
Equities, market total (FTSE UK)	9.5	14.1
10-year government bonds	8.6	3.2
Inflation	5.1	4.0

Sources: Investment Property Databank (IPD), Thomson DataStream (both accessed June 2008).

The annual average returns and standard deviation of these variables are included in Table 3.6. For the period 1979–2006 in the United Kingdom, real estate assets offered the best return as well as carrying less volatility than the stock market.

Direct investment versus equities and bonds in the USA

The profitability index for real estate, equities, bonds and the inflation rate for the period 1979–2006 in the USA is calculated in Figure 3.19. In this market, investment in equities offered higher annual returns than did direct investment in real estate. Real estate investment grew faster than bonds from 1997 onwards.

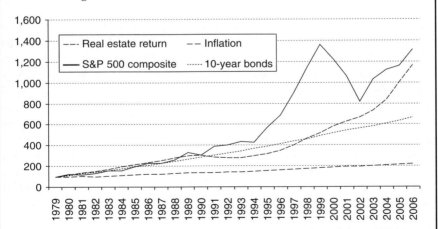

Figure 3.19 Cumulative returns on real estate direct investment and other asset classes, USA, 1979–2006 (December 1979 = 100)
Sources: NCREIF, Thomson DataStream (accessed June 2008).

In the USA, real estate investment had a lower risk than stocks and higher risk than bonds. As in the United Kingdom, all three asset classes had returns above the rate of inflation; see Table 3.7.

Table 3.7   Annual average returns and standard deviations of real estate, equities and bonds, USA, 1979–2006

	USA	
	Returns (%)	**Standard deviation (%)**
Equities, market total (S&P USA)	11.1	15.2
Direct real estate investment	9.7	6.1
10-year government bonds	7.3	2.8
Inflation	3	1.8

Sources: NCREIF, Thomson DataStream, (accessed June 2008).

Table 3.8   Correlation between direct real estate investment and investment in equities and bonds, United Kingdom and USA, 1980–2006

	Equities	**Bonds**
Direct real estate investment, United Kingdom	0.1952	−0.0998
Direct real estate investment, USA	0.0827	0.1611

Sources: Investment Property Databank (IPD), Thomson DataStream, (both accessed June 2008) and NCREIF.

Real estate investment has gradually gained market acceptance as a different asset class that has a strategic place in a diversified portfolio. Given their low correlation with equities and bonds, real estate assets are a good choice for diversifying the risk of an investment portfolio. The correlation coefficients for the United Kingdom and the USA are shown in Table 3.8. The proxies for stocks are the FTSE All Shares index for the United Kingdom and the S&P 500 index for the USA; 10-year government bonds are used for both countries.

As Table 3.8 shows, the correlation between the returns on direct real estate investment and other asset classes is very small in both countries, and for both asset classes. In the case of bonds, it becomes negative in the United Kingdom.

Property derivatives

The universe of investment alternatives has recently been further amplified with the introduction of property derivatives. Derivatives are not essentially direct investments but they replicate the direct investment results.

A property derivative is a financial instrument whose value is dependent on the value of an underlying real estate asset, usually represented in the form of an index. The underlying index could be a house price index or a commercial one, resulting in a residential or a commercial derivative. The property derivative market is an emerging market that is growing very fast, and shows the increasing integration of the real estate and capital markets. Property derivatives offer an alternative way of investing in commercial and residential property, as well as a mechanism for managing existing exposure in both the direct and the indirect markets. They enable strategic and tactical management of property market risk by gaining or reducing exposure to property without dealing in the physical asset or through indirect vehicles.

The development of a derivative market for direct real estate will now offer real estate investors many of the same risk management options that have been available to investors in stocks, bonds and commodities, such as hedging, risk management and portfolio re-allocation tools. In addition, it makes the international diversification and creation of long and short positions easier. The level of exposure in the property derivatives market is much more liquid than in the direct investment market and enables ownership costs to be avoided (that is, rental voids and maintenance expenses, management charges and estate agents' fees, stamp duty expenditure and legal costs).

The most relevant real estate derivatives are swaps, certificates/bonds and options (Deutsche Bank Research, 2007). *Real estate swap* deals are the most common. In these deals, the contracting parties swap cash flows, so to speak. For example, an investor who has a large real estate portfolio is able to reduce his/her exposure by entering into a total return swap. With such a deal, he or she locks into a fixed or floating rate of interest paid regularly. In exchange, the investor pays the counterparty the movements in a (total return) Property Index. In the event of a weakening real estate market the investor can stabilize the returns on his portfolio as the additional cash flow is kept relatively constant by the fixed rate (or euribor/libor plus a premium); see Figure 3.20.

Real estate bonds are based on the same idea. They are based on a certificate reflecting a property index. Based on this instrument the investor makes a real estate investment linked to the index.

At the time of writing, early experience is being gained with *real estate index options*. These options give the client the right to carry out a transaction at a later date, at a price that has been agreed. A call option may, for example, give the client the right to purchase an index-linked property product at the price previously agreed upon, giving the investor the

Figure 3.20   Property derivatives: the operation of a real estate total return swap

possibility of benefiting from a rising market. If the market drops, the investor does not exercise the option and loses only the premium. Conversely, an investor buying a put option can bet on a falling market, as he or she buys the right to sell an index-linked product at the price agreed.

In addition to the established products mentioned, *forward contracts* are possible. Here, the contracting parties commit themselves to carrying out a later transaction with the agreed conditions.

While residential property market far exceeds the commercial property market, the volume of the commercial property derivatives trade dwarfs residential volume. In the United Kingdom, the trade volume of commercial property derivatives on the United Kingdom IPD Index is growing in each quarter. The total notional of trades executed in the last quarter of 2007 was worth 1.7 billion pounds sterling, reaching a total outstanding notional 9 billion pounds sterling; see Figure 3.21. The residential property derivative market as a whole reached a 2 billon pound sterling outstanding balance in the first quarter of 2007 (Santander Global Banking and Markets).

There are an increasing number of commercial property indices, but property derivatives are not traded on all of them. The commercial property derivatives marketed in Europe are traded on some of the IPD indices (United Kingdom, France, Germany, Switzerland and Italy) and on the FTSE UK Commercial Property Index. Outside Europe, the market operates in the USA with the US-NCREIF as the underlying index, and in Japan and Australia with the IPD index. The United Kingdom has the most highly developed market in volume terms.

The Halifax's House Price Index (HPI) in the United Kingdom and the ZWEX residential market index in Switzerland are the only European indices on housing prices that are used as underlying indices for residential property derivatives. The following are also used as underlying indices for residential property derivatives: the S&P/Case-Shiller home price index in the USA, the Hong Kong Residential Price Index and the RP Data-Riskmark 'Hedonic' Property Price Index in Australia.

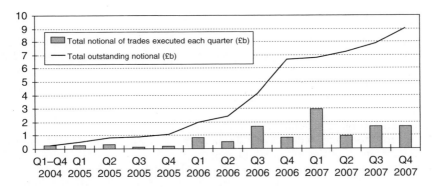

Figure 3.21 Trading volume of commercial property derivatives, United Kingdom, 2004–7 (UK IPD index; in billions of pounds sterling)
Source: IPD/IPF Trade Volume Report.

Property derivatives transactions in the USA

The monthly trading volume of residential property derivatives is fairly irregular in the USA; see Figure 3.22. The property derivatives market is less developed in the USA than in the United Kingdom.

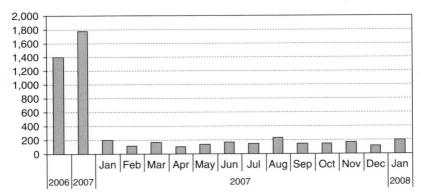

Figure 3.22 Trading volume of residential property derivatives, USA, 2006–January 2008 (millions of US dollars)
Note: Derivatives based on the S&P/Case-Shiller Index.
Source: Chicago Mercantile Exchange *Data Report* (various dates).

No information is available on the trading volume of commercial property derivatives based on the NCREIF Property Index.

Bibliography

Bigman, T. and Chiu, Ch. (2005) 'The Case for a Strategic Allocation to Global Real Estate Securities', *Morgan Stanley Investment Management Journal*, 2(2) (Fall).

Chicago Mercantile Exchange (various dates) *Data Report.*

Deutsche Bank Research (2007) *Property Derivatives Marching Across Europe* (12 June).

European Mortgage Federation (www.hypo.org)

European Mortgage Federation (2007) *Hypostat 2006: A Review of Europe's Mortgage and Housing Markets* (November).

Investment Property Databank (IPD). Available at www.ipd.com.

IPD/IPF Trade Volume Report (http://www.ipd.com/OurProducts/Indices/ DerivativesInformation/UKTradingVolumes/tabid/489/Default.aspx).

Jones Lang LaSalle (2005) *European Capital Markets Bulletin* (Full Year).

4
Indirect Investment in Real Estate: Listed Companies and Funds

There are two main vehicles for indirect investment in real estate: real estate investment funds and real estate companies. With these instruments, not only does the investor take a position in the real estate market, he or she also acquires different risk/return structures, which may vary according to the instrument being used.*

Indirect investment is alleged to have many advantages over direct investment. Some of the advantages are related to scale (indirect investment allows for smaller-sized investments); diversification (an investment in an indirect vehicle could lead to a share of the investment in huge and diversified portfolios); and professional management that helps investors to choose suitable stakes. Of course, there are also disadvantages of indirect investment; for example, quoted real estate companies could be affected by the general conditions in the stock markets in addition to the situation with the real estate assets themselves; and that real estate funds are often more opaque in their functioning.

There are many differences between real estate companies and investment funds; there is a continuing discussion about which is better at accommodating the investment of both households and institutional investors. Up to a point the discussion is worthless, since either could be the better choice depending on the investor's objectives and prerequisites, and, until very recently, both categories of vehicle benefited from a good availability of funds and performance. There has been sophistication on both sides, funds have developed an ever-better legal fit and tax frameworks, and adapted their investment policies to meet the needs of different segment of the investment community. Companies in many European countries achieved the possibility of adopting the legal form of real estate investment trusts – REITs.

---

* This chapter draws heavily on Suárez and Vassallo, 2005.

The companies analysed in this chapter are those quoted on stock markets. In some cases, when both indirect vehicle categories are compared, they are referred to as public vehicles (quoted companies) and private ones (funds). Quoted companies are traded daily and reflect the market conditions almost instantly, so they are affected directly by changes in the cycle in some sectors of the real estate industries in some countries – as was stated in previous chapters – and at the time of writing, the performance of several companies is deteriorating rapidly. So a downturn in the indices of real estate companies will be commented in this chapter – a drop of 32.2 per cent in Europe (ex-United Kingdom) in 2007, of 38.4 per cent in the United Kingdom, and of 19.6 per cent in the USA.

Another class of institutional investors are insurance companies and pension funds. While they are not properly indirect investment vehicles in real estate for households or other institutional investors, they are such relevant investors in real estate that they are studied – from that perspective – in an Appendix to this chapter (see pages 145–50). Both institutions have a small part of their investment portfolios allocated to real estate, with different policies among European countries that are significant, but just a small fraction of their huge portfolios and their variations could have a notable impact on real estate markets.

Listed real estate companies

Investment volume

As of January 2007, the 100 largest European listed real estate companies had an investment portfolio valued at 328 billion euros (up 44 per cent on the previous year), and a joint market capitalization of 153 billion euros (up 56 per cent on the previous year). By country of origin, the United Kingdom, France, the Netherlands, Spain and Italy have the largest volumes (Europe Real Estate, 2007); see Figure 4.1.

The difference between the United Kingdom investment volume, with 113 billion euros, and the other countries is notable. The British company, British Land, is the largest European real estate company, with an investment value of 25.5 billion euros in 2007, an increase of 4 billion euros over the previous year; see Table 4.1. In second place is Land Securities, also a British company, with 21 billion euros in real estate assets, an increase of 23 per cent over the previous year. These two companies invest only in the United Kingdom, and 90 per cent of their portfolio is invested in offices and shopping centres. In third place, with 15 billion euros, is Pirelli Real Estate, which experienced significant growth

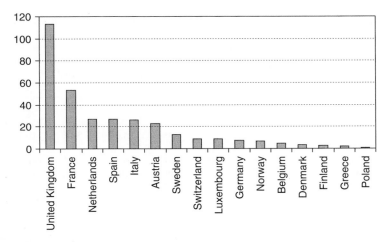

Figure 4.1   Investment volume by country of origin, 100 largest listed real estate companies, Europe, as at 1 January 2007 (in billions of euros)
Source: Europe Real Estate (2007).

in 2006. Pirelli's portfolio includes offices and, to a lesser extent, houses and shopping centres; it has operations in Germany and Poland, and plans to expand further in Central and Eastern Europe. In what follows, investment volume is equivalent to portfolio investment, and both are measured by the gross asset value of the entity.

In 2007, Metrovacesa was the fourth-largest company in Europe in investment volume. It too moved up several positions in the list, from 12th place in 2006. In March 2005, this company bought most of the shares of Gecina, which was in 6th place. The two companies' combined investment volume amounted to 23 billion euros. Metrovacesa has a diversified portfolio in offices, shopping centres, industrial property, hotels and residential real estate. In 2007, Metrovacesa and Gecina signed a demerger agreement.

The next company in the list is the Austrian company, IMMOFINANZ. Its business is focused primarily on the residential sector and, to a lesser extent, on offices and shopping centres. It is followed by Gecina from France, and Liberty International Group from the United Kingdom, which fell from 3rd place in 2006 to 7th place. Unibail, from France, and Rodamco Europe, from the Netherlands, reached a merger agreement in 2007. These two companies specialise primarily in shopping centres and offices.

Tenth place was held by Foncière des Régions. The previous year, it was in 45th place. It holds assets worth more than 14 billion euros, of

Table 4.1   Fifteen largest listed real estate companies, Europe, 1 January 2007
Ranked by investment volume. Figures in billions of euros

Company name	Country of origin	Investment volume	Market capitalization	Free float (%)	Premium/ discount (%)	Scope
British Land	UK	25.5	13.1	100	n.a.	National
Land Securities	UK	20.5	16.0	100	n.a.	National
Pirelli Real Estate	IT	15.0	2.0	n.a.	88.6	Multinational
Metrovacesa	SP	13.2	13.0	n.a.	141.2	National
IMMOFINANZ	AT	11.8	4.8	100	6.0	Multinational
Gecina	FR	10.6	9.0	20	16.3	National
Liberty International	UK	10.5	7.5	100	n.a.	National
Unibail	FR	10.2	1.0	100	32.5	National
Rodamco Europe	NL	9.9	9.0	75	22.1	Multinational
Foncière des Régions	FR	9.8	4.2	50	39.1	National
Hammerson	UK	8.9	6.6	100	n.a.	Multinational
GAGFAH	LU	8.1	5.4	20	138.5	National
Klépierre	FR	7.9	6.6	50	39	Multinational
Capital and Regional	UK	7.4	1.6	100	n.a.	National
IMMOEAST	AT	6.5	5.9	50	13.5	Multinational

Note: UK: United Kingdom; IT: Italy; SP: Spain; AT: Austria; FR: France; NL: Netherlands; LU: Luxembourg.
Sources: Ranking done by Europe Real Estate (2007) in co-operation with EPRA and Kempen & Co.

which 7 billion are invested in France, 4 billion in Italy and 3 billion in Germany. Its strong growth during 2006 was basically a result of its merger with Bail Investissement. It focuses on shopping centres and car parks.

The last five places in the list were held by Hammerson, GAGFAH, Klépierre, Capital and Regional, and IMMOEAST. Hammerson is a property investment and development company focusing on the retail and office sectors. GAGFAH is a management, ownership and acquisition company with a diversified residential portfolio throughout Germany. Klépierre is a property investment company focused on shopping centres in continental Europe and office buildings in Paris. Capital and Regional is a property investment and management company active in retail properties, mainly throughout the United Kingdom. Ranked 15th by investment volume is IMMOEAST, a subsidiary of IMMOFINANZ, this firm is active in different countries of Central and Eastern Europe.

By market capitalization, Land Securities takes first place, followed by British Land, Metrovacesa, Gecina, Rodamco Europe and United Kingdom Balance Property Trust (which, with a market capitalization of 8.4 billion euros, is a property investment trust specializing in commercial real estate in the United Kingdom). Seventh place is held by Liberty International, followed by Hammerson and Klépierre, from the United Kingdom and France, respectively. Both are focused on investment in and the development of shopping centres and offices. In the list ranked by investment volume, they hold 11th and 13th places, respectively. The 10th place in market capitalization is held by IMMOEAST.

Introduction of REIT equivalents in Europe

[Note: With regard to the data on the introduction of the REITs framework in various European countries, this section is based on EPRA (2007).]

In some European countries, real estate companies can adopt a legal status similar to that of a real estate investment trust – a REIT. REITs appeared in the USA following an amendment to a popular legislative landmark: the 1960 tax extension law on cigarettes/cigars. In fact, they date back to the nineteenth century – 1880, to be precise, when investors were able to avoid double taxation by using trusts, which were exempt from tax at corporate level if profits were shared among investors. In 1930, this tax advantage was abolished and any passive investments had to be declared by each investor, first at corporate level and, later, individually.

Demand from the industry led to the introduction of the 1960 Real Estate Investment Trust Act, which eliminated this double taxation, qualifying REITs as pass-through entities. In 1986, the Reform Act allowed REITs to manage their real estate directly; that is, they could exist without an intermediary management company. This eliminated many of the conflicts existing between REITs and their administrators. In 1993, the barriers preventing pension funds from investing in REITs were removed (see www.reitnet.com).

A REIT is a 'legal guise' used by real estate companies whose securities can be traded on a stock market. It is a property investment company, whose main activities are managing, letting or selling real estate, investing in other real estate companies, and even financing real estate. REITs are far more liquid than other alternative investment vehicles. They generally operate like any other real estate company; what makes them different is that they are exempt from corporate tax, provided their investment policies and income distribution (in the USA, 90 per cent of income) comply with the prevailing laws in each country. REIT regimes started to appear gradually in European countries.

The Netherlands

In 1969, BIs (*Fiscale Beleggingsinstelling*) appeared in the Netherlands, made possible by the Dutch Corporate Tax Act. The BI regime is a pure tax regime, and therefore any company wishing to adopt this legal form does not have to meet any legal requirements. BIs are listed on the securities market and as such come under the supervision of the Dutch Financial Market Authority. BIs must be devoted exclusively to portfolio investment activities and can only have a leverage of 60 per cent of the book value of the real property and 20 per cent of the book value of all other property. BIs must distribute 100 per cent of their operating income, while capital gains or losses are placed in a tax-free reserve, which does not have to be distributed. Profits must be distributed within eight months of the close of the financial year.

Belgium

In 1995, the SICAFI (*Société d'investissement à capital fixe en immobilière*) structure, a specific real estate investment institution having favourable tax treatment, was created in Belgium. A SICAFI is defined as 'a listed property fund, with a fixed amount of corporate share capital, whose role is to provide tax neutrality for collecting and distributing the rental income' (EPRA (2007). Under Belgian law, SICAFIs must have a specific legal status which includes a suitable corporate form: limited liability company, or limited partnership with shares. The company must be resident in Belgium, have a minimum shareholders' equity of 1.25 million euros and be incorporated for an unlimited period of time. The portfolio directors and managers must also have appropriate professional experience.

SICAFIs may have leverage of 65 per cent of the company's assets at the time the loan agreement is concluded; the annual interest cost may not exceed 80 per cent of the total annual profit. They must distribute 80 per cent of their net profit in the form of dividends. Capital gains do not have to be distributed and remain tax-free, provided they are reinvested within the following four years. Profits must be distributed on an annual basis.

France

In France, at the end of 2003, the SIIC (*Société d'investissement immobilier cotée*) tax regime was created, which comes under the supervision of the Autorité des Marchés Financiers. Any listed real estate investment company, or any subsidiary whose capital is at least 95 per cent held by the parent company, may adopt this legal form. A SIIC's main activity must be passive investment in the real estate industry, as well direct or indirect portfolio investments in partnerships and companies with similar activities and goals to SIIC. Other ancillary activities, such as real property development or brokerage, are also permitted, but they may not account for more than 20 per cent of the company's gross assets, and income from these activities would be fully taxable. Financial leasing of properties entered into before 2005 is permitted but may not account for more than 50 per cent of the company's gross assets. However, if the SIIC parent company or subsidiary entered after the year 2005, this activity is considered an eligible activity.

Unlimited leverage is permitted. SIICs must distribute 85 per cent of profit from real estate leasing before the end of the tax year following the year in which they are generated, also the 100 per cent of the dividends received by any subsidiary that has opted for the SIIC regime. Fifty percent of capital gains arising from the transfer of real assets or the shares of real estate companies, as well as from the shares of any subsidiary companies that have opted for the SIIC structure, must be distributed.

Since SIICs were introduced in France, the country's real estate companies have experienced dramatic growth. They went from a stock market capitalization of 10 billion euros when the SIICs were introduced, to 47.8 billion in January 2007, and paying significant dividends. The FTSE/EPRA/NAREIT index for France returned 204 per cent between 2002 (very close to the introduction of SIICs) and December 2007, adjusted for dividends and capital increases, well above the return of the European (118.3 per cent) and Global FTSE/EPRA/NAREIT (112.9 per cent) real estate indices. Currently, all the major listed real estate companies have adopted the SIIC structure, including Gecina, Klépierre and Unibail, mentioned earlier. Since SIICs were first introduced, new players have entered the market, and foreign investment in the sector has increased notably.

Germany

G-REITs were introduced in Germany on 1 January 2007. To obtain this status, a company had to be registered in the Companies Registry and meet certain requirements, such as: to be a joint stock company with a minimum share capital of 15 million euros; have its corporate headquarters and management in Germany; comply with certain provisions; and be listed. At least 75 per cent of its assets must consist of real estate (immovable property) and at least 75 per cent of its gross earnings

REITs in North America, Asia-Pacific and Africa

REIT regimes also exist in other countries, including Australia (the LPT, Limited Property Trust, since 1985) and South Africa (the PUT). The LPT and the PUT are highly successful tax transparency vehicles which have been a far-reaching investment stimulus in their markets. In Asia-Pacific, J-REITs have existed in Japan since the year 2000, and REIC in South Korea since 2001. Hong Kong has had REITs since 2003, and S-REITs have existed in Singapore since 1999. Canada has had MFTs (Canadian REITs) since 1993.

Table 4.2 shows the spread of REITs outside Europe.

Table 4.2   REIT regimes in North America, Asia-Pacific and Africa, February 2008

Country	Enacted	Market Capitalization (US$billions)	Number of REITs	Structure
North America				
USA	1960	312	152	REIT
Canada	1994	27	16	MFT
Asia-Pacific				
Australia	1985	97	23	LPT
Japan	2000	96	23	J-REIT
South Korea	2001	0.5+	6	REIC
Singapore	1999	20.8	11	SREIT
Hong Kong	2003	5.4	21	HK-REIT

Sources: FTSE/EPRA/NAREIT Index; EPRA (2007).

must come from the rental, leasing, letting and disposal of immovable property.

A G-REIT can only perform secondary activities through ownership of 100 per cent of the share capital of a REIT service company. Furthermore, a G-REIT must not undertake property selling. Investment in residential immovable property is prohibited if the property is in Germany and was built before 1 January 2007. Its leverage is limited to 55 per cent of the book value of the immovable property. It must distribute 90 per cent of its annual net income; deferral of 50 per cent of the capital gains is allowed.

Italy

A new real estate investment regime, SIIQ (*Società d'Intermediazione Quotate*), of Italian listed real estate investment corporations, was created in Italy in December 2006. It is the new REIT regime and may be considered as a supplement to the pre-existing real estate investment fund regime, the REIF. For an Italian real estate company to be able to take on this legal form, which still has a number of points to be defined, it must be a joint stock corporation (*Società per Azioni*), it must include the name SIIQ, and it must be regulated by the Italian Code of Commerce.

The company must have a minimum share capital of 40 million euros, 80 per cent of its assets must consist of property, and 80 per cent of its revenues must come from real estate rental and leasing activities. For the moment, there are no constraints on leverage for these companies. The SIIQ must distribute 85 per cent of its operating income from real estate rental and leasing. It must also distribute the dividends received from its investments in other SIIQs. The requirements as regards distribution of capital gains have not yet been defined.

United Kingdom

In the United Kingdom, as in Germany, the regime for UK REITs came into force in January 2007. Since their introduction, several listed British real estate companies have taken this legal form. For a property company to become a UK REIT, it must be a listed, closed-ended property company tax resident in the United Kingdom. This company may have non-resident subsidiaries but they will probably not enjoy the benefits of fiscal transparency. The company must have a minimum share capital of 50,000 pounds sterling, not because this is imposed by the UK REIT regime but because these are requirements of the London Stock Exchange.

With regard to its business activity, the constraints are imposed by what is called the 'Balance of Business Test', which requires that 75 per cent of the net income is drawn from the property rental business, and that at least 75 per cent of its assets are invested in the property rental business. In essence, only the income from real estate in the United Kingdom will be tax exempt. There is no limit on the real estate assets that they may be held, but the company must have at least three distinct assets, none of which may exceed 40 per cent of the total. UK REITs may also invest abroad.

The leverage is limited by the interest coverage ratio, earnings before interest and taxes (EBIT)/interest charge on debt, the result should not fall below 1.25 for an accounting period. Ninety per cent of the

Table 4.3 Tax treatment of the different REIT-like legal frameworks in Europe

	Current income	**Capital gains**	**Withholding tax**
The Netherlands (BI)	Real estate income is included in the tax exemption and is taxed at 0%	Capital gains or losses are allocated to a tax-free reserve and are therefore exempt from tax	Taxes withheld are refunded
Belgium (SICAFI)	The eligible rental income is excluded from the taxable basis	Capital gains are not included in taxable profit	15% dividend withholding tax, which may be reduced pursuant to application of tax treaties
France (SIIC)	Fully exempt from corporate tax: • income from qualifying leasing activities • Dividends received from qualifying subsidiaries	Eligible capital gains tax-exempt	In principle, domestic sourced income not subject to withholding tax The taxes withheld on foreign sourced income could be credited if a double tax treaty allows
Germany (G-REIT)	All income is tax-exempt	Capital gains are tax-exempt	Exemption or refund
Italy (SIIQ)	Eligible income is tax-exempt	Ordinary corporate taxation	n.a.
United Kingdom (UK REIT)	Rental income from tax-exempt property no subject to tax Non-tax-exempt business is taxable in the ordinary way (30%)	Eligible property is tax-exempt	In principle, no withholding tax levied on domestic distributions (only on tax-exempt profit distributions) If foreign income is taxable, credit of foreign withholding tax is possible

Source: EPRA (2007).

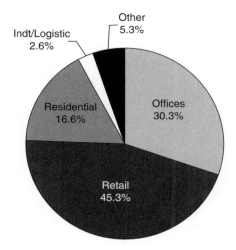

Figure 4.2 Portfolio composition, fifteen largest companies by investment volume, Europe, 1 January 2007 (as percentages of total portfolio)
Note: Of the fifteen largest companies, five are from the United Kingdom, four from France, two from Austria, one from the Netherlands, one from Spain, one from Italy and one from Luxembourg.
Source: Europe Real Estate (2007).

tax-exempt rental income must be distributed to the shareholders within twelve months after the end of the business year. On the other hand, capital gains from property sales need not be distributed. However, if the gains are not reinvested within two years, they will be considered a 'bad asset' under the 'Balance of Business Test' at the asset level.

Table 4.3 sums up the tax treatment given to the different REIT regimes in Europe.

Investment characteristics: types of assets and debts

At the end of 2006, most of the investment by the largest property companies was in retail premises, with 45.3 per cent of the portfolio, followed by offices, with 30.3 per cent; see Figure 4.2. For the fifteen largest companies, investment in retail assets has been variable in recent years, from 33.4 per cent at the end of 2004 and 38.8 per cent at the end of 2005 to 45.3 per cent in 2007. The investment in offices fell from 46.4 per cent and 35.2 per cent at the ends of 2004 and 2005, respectively, to 30.3 per cent in 2007. In addition to the increase in the retail sector, the fall in investment in offices has been offset by

Table 4.4 Portfolio composition, fifteen largest property companies, Europe, January 2007 (percentages by investment category)

	Origin	Offices	Retail	Residential	Industrial/ logistics	Other
British Land	UK	36	61			3
Land Securities	UK	40	56			4
Pirelli Real Estate	IT	47	12	17	7	17
Metrovacesa	SP	41	6	42	3	8
IMMOFINANZ	AT	23	16	40	11	11
Gecina	FR	55		40		5
Liberty International	UK	14	86			
Unibail	FR	30	53			17
Rodamco Europe	NL	5	93			1
Foncière des Régions	FR	78				
Hammerson	UK	29	71			
GAGFAH	LU			96		4
Klépierre	FR	12	88			
Capital and Regional	UK		100			
IMMOEAST	AT	38	28	12	14	8

Note: AT: Austria; FR: France; IT: Italy; LU: Luxembourg; NL: Netherlands; SP: Spain; UK: United Kingdom.
Source: Europe Real Estate Yearbook (2007).

the residential sector, whose investment percentage more than doubled, from 7.5 per cent in 2005 to 16.6 per cent in 2007.

The individual company portfolios differ widely: while some companies are close to the average, others are overweight in some asset classes – for example, companies such as Metrovacesa, IMMOFINANZ, Gecina or GAGFAH, that allocate significant investment percentages to the residential sector; see Table 4.4. Foncière des Régions are above the average in offices, while Rodamco Europe, Klépierre, and Capital and Regional concentrate more on retail assets.

The average leverage of the fifteen largest companies is 46.2 per cent, measured as total debt related to total debt plus shareholders' equity. Two of the more leveraged companies are Metrovacesa and Foncière des Régions, companies that have been involved in merger and acquisitions processes; see Figure 4.3.

Another view of the leverage of property companies is offered by the loan-to-value ratio. In this parameter, the property companies'

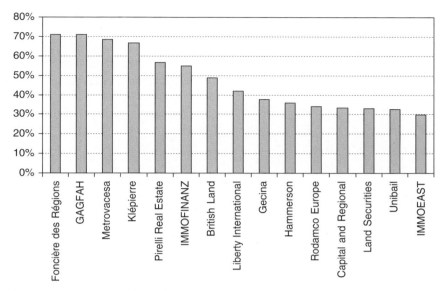

Figure 4.3 Leverage of the fifteen largest European real estate companies by investment volume, 31 December 2006 (total debt/(total debt + shareholders' equity))
Sources: Europe Real Estate Yearbook (2007); Thomson DataStream (accessed June 2008).

positioning is very similar to that shown in Figure 4.4, with Metrovacesa, GAGFAH and Foncière des Régions holding the top places.

Stock market performance of listed real estate companies

It has been stated that real estate stocks performance has two components, one related to the stock markets in general and the other to the evolution of the property markets themselves. The comparison of the property companies in relation to the stock market put into perspective the nature of real estate investment. Figure 4.5 shows the performance of European real estate stocks (represented by the EPRA indices) *vis-à-vis* the general European stock markets (represented by the FTSE). Between 1996 and the beginning of 2000, the returns on the FTSE were above the EPRA real estate index, reflecting investors' preference for industries that are considered to be more dynamic, such as those related to the new technologies. After 2000, with the stock market crisis, almost all the stocks fell in value, while the real estate companies acted as 'safe haven' stocks; the only falls in this sector in those years were in the United Kingdom. All indices began to increase after 2003, with a clear lead in the case of the real estate companies of Europe, excluding the United Kingdom.

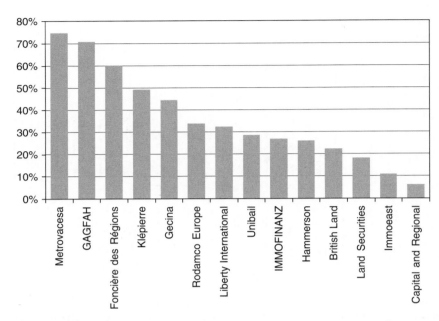

Figure 4.4   Loan-to-value ratio, fifteen largest property companies by invest-ment volume, Europe, 31 December 2006 (total debt/gross asset value)
Note: Pirelli RE is not included in this Figure because of its combination of owned and managed assets.
Sources: Europe Real Estate Yearbook (2007); Thomson DataStream (accessed June 2008).

By early 2007, the consequences of the slowdown of the real estate market were starting to become apparent. During 2007, the return of the EPRA Europe index (excluding the United Kingdom) fell by 32.2 per cent, the first year of negative growth in more than a decade, and EPRA UK fell by 38.4 per cent.

Real estate investment funds in Europe

Real estate investment funds are unincorporated collective investment institutions. Savings drawn from the public are deposited in a fund to be used basically to purchase property, which is then let in order to obtain a return. They differ enormously depending on the types of investors they are aimed at. Funds aimed at the general public are subject to strict monitoring by a government body and are classed as 'Retail', while those aimed at a privately controlled group of companies, which are not subject to any public monitoring, are classed as 'Private' or 'Private equity'.

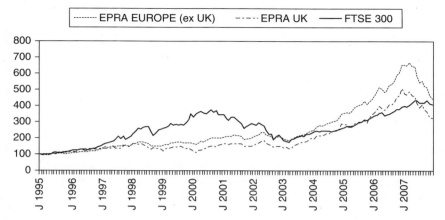

Figure 4.5 Returns on real estate stocks and the general stock market, Europe, 1995–2007 (EPRA Europe excluding the United Kingdom, EPRA UK and FTSE 300; in local currencies)
Note: Indices are rebased, January 1995 = 100.
Source: Thomson DataStream (accessed June 2008).

Real estate funds can be closed-ended funds, or closed funds, when they have a limited life and a specific investment volume that does not fluctuate over time; that is, if one investor wishes to disinvest, he/she must sell the stake because the fund will not sell it for him/her, which is why these funds have an initial capital collection period. Vehicles with this structure are normally aimed at institutional investors, and their activity is regulated by their own rules. These funds are most common for riskier-than-average investments because they do not adapt easily to disinvestment and therefore require capital to be committed for a certain period of time in order to achieve their objectives (ABN-AMRO/IPD, 2003).

On the other hand, open funds, or open-ended funds, do not have a limited life and are always open to new investment, so their assets increase and/or decrease over time. Of the total funds in the INREV (European Association of Investors in Non-Listed Real Estate Vehicles) database as of January 2007, 204 were open-ended, with a gross asset value (GAV) of 203.2 billion euros, and 286 were closed-ended, with a GAV of 125.7 billion euros (INREV Vehicles Database).

Concerning the investment styles, real estate investment funds can be classified into three categories: core or nuclear; core-plus or value-added; and opportunity. *Core funds* invest in low-risk real estate assets and have a low financial leverage, if any. They normally aim at returns up to 11.5 per cent. The majority of vehicles in the United Kingdom and Germany use this style of investment (ABN-AMRO/IPD, 2003).

The comparison of real estate stocks returns and the general stock market in the United States paints a similar picture to that in Europe. The periods during which the listed real estate companies offered higher returns than the stock markets coincided with Europe. However, the range of variation in the returns offered was greater in Europe, which suggests that the European market had greater volatility in monthly terms. In the case of the US market, the cumulative return of the real estate sector did not overtake that of the general stock market until 2006 and that was to be short-lived; see Figure 4.6. The fall in the stock prices of the listed real estate companies in 2007 has had a global impact, with the property companies being the hardest hit, the EPRA/NAREIT-USA fell by 19.6 per cent in that year.

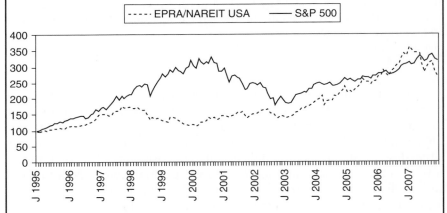

Figure 4.6 Returns on real estate stocks and the general stock market, USA, 1995–2007 (EPRA/NAREIT USA and S&P 500; in local currency)
Note: Indices are rebased, January 1995 = 100.
Source: Thomson Datastream (accessed June 2008).

Core-plus or value-added funds invest in medium-risk real estate assets and usually have a financial leverage of between 30 per cent and 70 per cent of the gross asset value of the portfolio. The main difference between core-plus funds and core funds is that the investment strategy of the former focuses more on capital growth, and the expected returns are between 11.5 per cent and 17 per cent. These two investment styles are the ones normally used by retail-investor funds.

Finally, *opportunity or opportunistic funds* invest in high-risk assets and have high levels of financial leverage, in excess of 60 per cent. In their

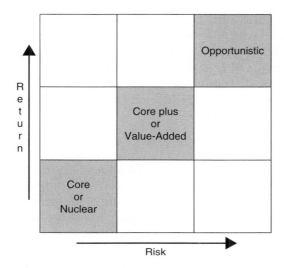

Figure 4.7   Real estate investment fund management styles

investment strategy, they place equal emphasis on capital growth and performance; the required returns tend to be between 17 per cent and 25 per cent. Some examples of investment in this type of fund are asset renewal or updating opportunities, usually with intensive management characteristics (ABN-AMRO/IPD, 2003). Figure 4.7 summarizes the different types of fund described above.

In each country, real estate funds have a special name and legal treatment. Some of them are tax transparent.

National characteristics of real estate funds

[Note: Most of this section is based on the publications from the INREV Vehicles Database.]

Italy

In 1994, FIIs (*Fondi di investimento immobiliare*) were introduced in Italy. They are investment funds that invest exclusively in immovable assets, rights in immovable assets and shareholdings in real estate companies. They are not legal entities, but rather pools of investment owned jointly by the unit holders. Unit holders pay taxes only when a profit is distributed or when they sell their units.

FIIs are tax-exempt and are managed by a management company, called a '*Società di gestione del risparmio*' (SGR). They can have a leverage of 60 per cent of the value of the real estate and 20 per cent of the value of other assets, and are under no obligation to distribute operating profit or capital gains. FIIs' revenues and capital gains are tax-exempt, but subject to withholding tax of 12.5 per cent, which may be reduced to 0 per cent where profits are distributed to qualified resident or non-resident unit holders. FIIs are not permitted to lend money or to invest in financial instruments issued by the SGR.

Austria

In Austria, 2003 saw the emergence of *Immobilien Investmentfonds* (IIFs). IIFs have no independent legal status and are administered by a management company, which acts in favour of the fund's investors. IIFs are tax transparent, which means that investors are treated for tax purposes as if they had invested directly in real estate, and so must pay 25 per cent withholding tax. This treatment is only given to qualified IIFs, which are defined as entities that can invest only in real estate.

These funds are limited to a leverage of 20 per cent of the market value of the fund's assets, or 40 per cent for special IIFs. There are no mandatory ratios for dividend payout, rental income or capital gains.

Germany

In Germany, the most common real estate fund is the open-ended real estate investment fund (*Offene Immobilienfonds – IFs*), introduced in 1969. Because of their relative importance, they will be addressed in greater detail in the next section. IFs are income-tax-exempt, provided the income consists of dividends received, capital gains on the disposal of shares in companies, and income from foreign and national real estate. This means there is a degree of transparency. In this case, investors are treated as if they received the income from an equity investment, rather than from a real estate investment. Withholding tax of 31.65 per cent is payable.

IFs do not have to be listed, and at least 5 per cent and no more than 49 per cent of their investments must be in liquid assets. Also, they are not allowed to invest more than 15 per cent of their assets in any one property. Leverage is limited to 50 per cent of the fair market value of the fund's property. These funds have no obligation to pay dividends.

Luxembourg

Since 1988, Luxembourg has had certain rules for undertakings for collective investment (UCIs) whose purpose is real estate investment: the real estate UCIs or REIFs (Real Estate Investment Funds). These vehicles may take two forms:

- *Fonds Commun de Placement* (FCP) is an indivisible fund administered by a management company that has no independent legal status. To form an FCP, the fund must have net assets of at least 1,250,000 euros. These vehicles are tax transparent; that is, apart from 'capital duty', they are tax-free in Luxembourg.
- *Société d'investissement à capital variable/fixe* (SICAV/SICAF), is legally a corporation and may be self-managed or managed by a management company. SICAV/SICAFs are tax opaque.

In a REIF, leverage must not exceed 50 per cent of the fund's total assets, and there is no obligation to distribute profits.

Spain

In Spain, there are real estate funds called FIIs (*Fondos de Inversión Inmobiliaria*) and real estate investment companies SIIs (*Sociedades de Inversión Inmobiliaria*). Both are subject to corporate taxes, although under certain conditions they may apply a reduced rate of 1 per cent. SIIs are corporations, whereas FIIs have no independent legal status; for legal purposes they are mutual funds. Both must have a minimum capital of 9,015,181.56 euros and at least 100 individual or institutional shareholders or unit holders. Neither has an obligation to be listed, although SIIs may opt for a stock market listing, whereas FIIs may not.

FIIs and SIIs may only invest in urban real estate for rental purposes. Leverage is limited to 50 per cent; there is no mandatory profit distribution; and withholding tax of 15 per cent is payable.

France

In France, the government launched a new legal structure for real estate investment in January 2007, in addition to the recently created SIICs, to be called OPCI (*Organismes de Placement Collectif Immobilier*). OPCIs were intended to replace SCPIs (*Sociétés civiles de placement immobilier*), which had been subject to many restrictions that prevented them from developing, but in contrast to what was initially announced, SCPIs will not be obliged to become OPCIs.

An OPCI is an open-ended real estate vehicle that benefits from fiscal transparency, like the SIIC. The OPCIs are divided into two types of vehicle, both of which are regulated by the financial market authorities (AMF – *Autorité des marchés financiers*):

- SPPICV (*Société de placement à prépondérante immobilière à capital variable*), which is considered a SICAV (*Société d'investissement à capital variable*) for legal purposes, and which will be exempt from corporation tax provided it distributes 85 per cent of the profits and 50 per cent of the capital gains. This vehicle is designed for retail investors, who will pay tax on the dividends received.

With respect to its assets, 60 per cent must be invested either directly or indirectly in real estate and 10 per cent in liquid cash assets. The remaining 30 per cent can be invested in many other ways. These vehicles have a maximum leverage of 50 per cent of the value of their assets.

- The OPCI RFA (*Règle de fonctionnement allégé*), also called FPI (*Fonds de placement immobilier*). These vehicles are companies that do not have a separate legal personality and benefit from fiscal transparency provided that they distribute 85 per cent of their net income. This vehicle is designed specifically for institutional investors, who will have to pay tax if the income they receive comes directly from real estate.

They are flexible vehicles, as there is no limit on the amount of leverage, management incentives are possible and the level of liquidity has to be limited only during the first three months of operations. There are two subcategories:

- o 'OPCI RFA Sans Effet de Levier (RFA SEL): in which no gearing is permitted but which benefits from loosened functioning rules; and
- o OPCI RFA avec Effet de Levier (RFA EL): in which gearing is permitted and functioning rules are less limited (INREV, 2007).

German open-ended funds

It is worth pointing out that, whereas in other European countries listed property companies play a very important role in the indirect real estate investment market, in Germany that role is played by real estate funds, specifically by the German open-ended funds (*Offene Immobilienfonds*), introduced briefly in the previous section (see page 130). The total volume of 103 billion euros mentioned before compares with the total stock market capitalization of listed real estate companies in Germany of 10 billion euros. German open-ended funds have a strong tradition in Europe and manage very significant volumes of assets compared to other European funds. German open-ended funds are private, indirect real estate investment vehicles with no predetermined life, and are always open to new investment and sales or depreciation, except where this is impossible for legal reasons. For this reason, the size of these investments varies over time.

The funds are managed by special investment management companies (*Kapitalanlagegesellschaft*), most of which are owned by German commercial banks, which use their extensive networks of contacts as a distribution channel for the funds' products. The key factor in these funds is their management of illiquid long-term assets and liquid short-term liabilities. They must invest in buildings, certain types of shares in real estate companies, and fixed income instruments (Maurer *et al.*, 2004).

There are currently 32 German open-ended funds (GOEs) in the INREV database, with 106 billion euros of assets invested. They are divided into three groups, based on the degree of geographical diversification: domestic funds, which invest only in Germany; European funds, which invest in other European countries as well as in Germany; and global funds, which invest at world level as well as in Germany. All these funds are public funds aimed at the individual saver.

The behaviour of these German funds is strongly linked to the geographical location of the investments: the higher the percentage of international investment (outside Germany), the stronger the performance. Domestic funds do not give very good returns, because the poor situation of the real estate industry in Germany (IXIS AEW Europe, Research and Strategy).

German open-ended funds are among the European funds that have grown most in recent years; in fact, they were one of the best vehicles in the world for collecting real estate capital, amassing around 14 billion euros in 2003. However, the capital flow invested in these funds decreased in 2004 to around 3 billion euros as a result of deterioration in their performance. Average performance dropped from 5.4 per cent in 2001 to 4.7 per cent in 2002, and then to 3.5 per cent by the middle of 2003. More recently, some alleged mismanagement led to the first mass withdrawals in fifteen years. German funds have to sell assets in order to offer their investors due performance, within the constraint that the law does not allow assets to be sold for less than their book value (Piserra, 2005: 54).

Main characteristics of real estate funds in Europe

The European non-listed real estate funds registered in INREV have grown in quantity and volume invested. Despite having a good level of new funds each year since 1995, the number launched has decreased in recent years; see Figure 4.8. In 2004, the INREV database included 119 new funds, with an increase of the total GAV amounting to 74 billion euros. This growth fell by half during 2005, with the launch of 60 new funds and an increase in the GAV of 36 billion euros. In 2006, new fund

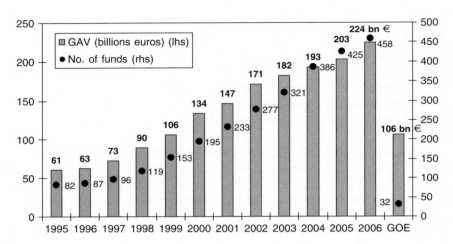

Figure 4.8   Non-listed real estate funds, Europe, 1995–2006 (cumulative gross asset value and no. of vehicles)

Note: GAV of GOE (German open-ended funds) is not included in GAV and year 2006.

Source: INREV, IPD (January 2007).

launches once again halved but the increase in GAV was very similar to that of the previous year, at 32 billion euros.

Among the 490 funds in the INREV database in December 2006, with a gross asset value of 330 billion euros, there were 258 core funds, 143 value-added and 57 opportunity funds. The 32 remaining funds were German open-ended funds (GOE), which amounted to a noteworthy 32 per cent of the total see Figure 4.9. The core funds have the larger portion of assets under management: 41 per cent. Their GAV is superior to that of the GOEs, but not substantially so, despite being far more numerous. They are followed by the value-added funds, with 17 per cent; and the opportunity funds, with 10 per cent. The latter also account for a significant proportion of total gross asset value, in proportion to the number of funds they represent.

Real estate investment funds can invest at national or international level. The majority of funds invest at national level (see Figure 4.10), but both the number of funds and the GAV they invest worldwide increase each year. In fact, the highest growth rate has come from international investments encouraged by the enhanced transparency and the growth of the size of the funds themselves. The largest funds investing on an international scale spread their portfolio over several countries in Western Europe, or across the whole continent.

The amount invested by single-country vehicles, and the target countries, are shown in Table 4.5. Clearly, the most investment by far is made

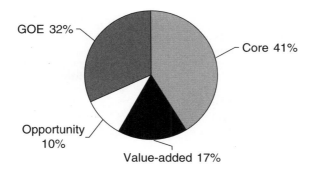

Figure 4.9   Real estate investment funds according to investment style, Europe, May 2006 (gross asset value)
Source: INREV, IPD (January 2007).

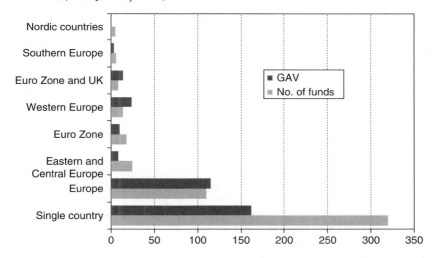

Figure 4.10   Geographical destinations of European fund investment, January 2007 (gross asset value (GAV); in billions of euros)
Note: Single-country funds invest over 75 per cent of their capital in a single country.
Source: INREV, IPD (January 2007).

in the United Kingdom. Within the investment of the single-country funds in this country, 26.7 billion euros is invested in the retail sector, 10.3 in offices, 6.9 in the industrial sector, 1.6 billions in residential and the rest in other diversified assets. The second largest country receiving a considerable volume of single-country investment, is Switzerland, followed by the Netherlands and Italy.

Concerning the funds' asset allocation, of the 490 funds in the INREV database as of December 2006, 283 had a diversified strategy and

Table 4.5   Country of investment, single-country funds, January 2007 (gross asset value (GAV) in billion of euros)

	GAV (billions euros)
1. United Kingdom	105.3
2. Switzerland	16.5
3. The Netherlands	10.7
4. Italy	8.0
5. Germany	6.3
6. Portugal	5.0
7. France	3.9
8. Spain	2.9
9. Norway	1.6
10. Austria	0.5
11. Denmark	0.4
12. Ireland	0.3
13. Finland	0.1
14. Sweden	0.1

Source: INREV, IPD (January 2007).

accounted for 71 per cent of the gross asset value (232.2 billion euros); see Figure 4.11. In addition to this, 58 funds were invested in retail properties, accounting for 12 per cent of the GAV (39.1 billion euros); 64 specialized in offices, accounting for 9 per cent (30.3 billion euros); 45 specialized in the residential market, 3 per cent of total GAV (11.1 billion euros); and 29 were invested in the industrial sector, accounting for 3 per cent (9.8 billion euros).

INREV studied the financial gearing of 206 real estate funds investing in Europe with a total net asset value of 153 billion euros. There are two categories in the index: funds that invest domestically (national – more than 75 per cent of their assets are invested in the same country) and multi-country funds (that invest less than 75 per cent of their assets in any single country). A further category is established, dividing them all into funds aimed at individual (retail vehicles) or institutional investors (institutional vehicles) (INREV, January 2008).

Table 4.6 shows the level of financial gearing in national (single-country) and multi-country (investment in any single country below 75 per cent) funds and, among these, in the subgroups of funds aimed at private (retail vehicles) or other investors (institutional vehicles). The level of financial gearing is defined as the face value of the debt as a percentage of the gross asset value of the fund. The levels of financial

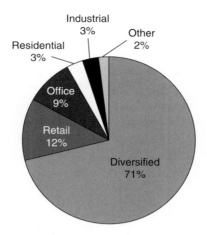

Figure 4.11 Investment portfolio of real estate funds, Europe, December 2006 (percentages of gross asset value)
Source: IPD INREV (January 2007).

Table 4.6 Financial gearing, European real estate funds, 2004–06

National/ Multi-country	Debt as a percentage of gross asset value (GAV)		
	2004	2005	2006
France	–	36.4	36.2
Germany	–	–	22.1
Institutional v.	–	–	39.5
Retail v.	–	–	–
Italy	17.6	9.9	21.8
Netherlands	37.3	28.6	27.2
Norway	–	–	23.2
Switzerland	20.7	15.7	15.8
Institutional v.	0.0	6.9	0.0
Retail v.	21.6	16.9	15.8
United Kingdom	14.5	14.9	14.6
Multi-country	26.6	25.0	19.2
Institutional v.	53.3	44.5	42.9
Retail v.	23.6	22.3	14.1

Note: v. = vehicles.
Source: *INREV Index Consultation Release* (January 2008).

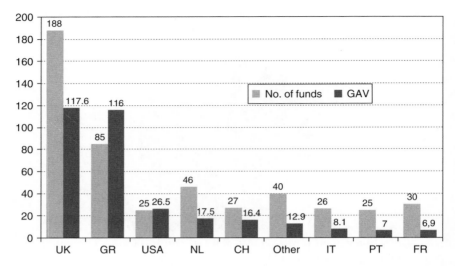

Figure 4.12 Country of origin, managing companies of real estate investment funds, Europe, December 2006 (gross asset value (GAV); in billions of euros and number of vehicles)
Source: INREV (January 2008).

gearing in these vehicles are not very high. The average financial gearing including all funds is 22.5 per cent, but when retail vehicles are excluded this average rises to 27.7 per cent. Funds aimed at institutional investors assume higher levels of debt, as they are aiming to achieve higher returns.

Single-country investment funds have higher levels of financial gearing than those investing internationally: the former borrow 23 per cent of their gross asset value and the latter, 19.2 per cent.

The largest real estate funds and fund managers

The United Kingdom is the country with the largest number of real estate fund managers; see Figure 4.12. Germany has far fewer fund managers than the United Kingdom, but in spite of this, the gross asset value managed by firms in both countries is quite similar. By levels of GAV, these would be followed by firms in the USA, the Netherlands and Switzerland.

As of December 2006, the vehicle with the highest GAV in the INREV database was *Haus Invest Europa* of Germany; see Figure 4.13. It was launched in 1972, making it one of the oldest funds in this market. It is an open-ended, core fund and is managed by Commerz Grundbesitz Investmentgesellschaft. Its targeted investor profile is retail, and its strategy is based on investing in Europe (Austria, Belgium, France,

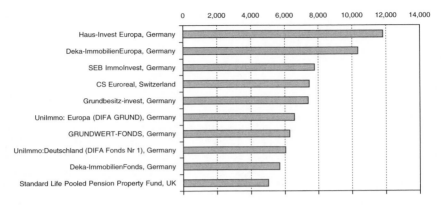

Figure 4.13 Ten largest real estate investment funds, Europe, December 2006 (gross asset value; in millions of euros)
Source: INREV (January 2008).

Germany, Italy, the Netherlands, Portugal, Spain, Sweden and the United Kingdom), and in diversified assets.

In second place was *Deka-Immobilien Europa* of Germany. This was launched in 1997, is an open-ended fund and therefore of unlimited duration. The fund is managed by Deka Immobilien Investment of Germany. It pursues a core investment strategy, aimed at retail investors. The fund has a global investment strategy, although most of its assets are invested in Europe (89 per cent), spread across different sectors. It has investments in Austria, Belgium, France, Germany, Hungary, the Republic of Ireland, Italy, Japan, Luxembourg, the Netherlands, Poland, Spain, Sweden, the United Kingdom and the USA.

Third place was taken by to *SEB ImmoInvest*, also from Germany. Launched in 1989, it is also an open-ended fund. It is managed by SEB Immobilien-Investment GmbH from Germany, which has a core investment strategy aimed mainly at retail investors. The fund's investments strategy is global, though most of its assets are invested in Europe (76 per cent): Belgium, France, Germany, Hungary, Italy, Luxembourg, the Netherlands, Spain, Sweden, and in the USA, diversifying via investment in different sectors.

Fund performance analysis

In 2006, the funds that invested at least 75 per cent of their portfolio in Norway offered the highest return, followed by those funds that invested in France, the United Kingdom and the Netherlands; see Figure 4.14. Europe All Vehicles, which is a weighted average of

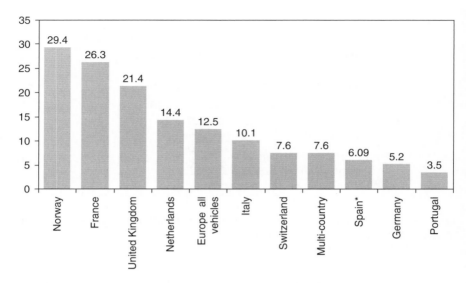

Figure 4.14 Single- and multi-country fund index returns, Europe, 2006 (annual performance; in local currencies; percentages)

Note: Based on 206 European funds, 128 at national level and 78 multi-country funds. The INREV indices were unfrozen indices at the time of going to print and therefore subject to change. *Spain is not included in Europe All Vehicles.

Sources: IPD *INREV Index* (January 2008); and INVERCO.

all of the funds included, had a return of 12.5 per cent. Below this mean, there were the funds operating in Italy and Switzerland, which at least were above the multi-country funds. The return provided by the multi-country funds only exceeds those of the Spanish, German and Portuguese funds.

The funds that invest at least 75 per cent of their portfolio in the United Kingdom present the highest return for the latest 3-year and 5-year periods at the time of writing, within the countries with available data. See Table 4.7 for the geometric mean of the returns for 2002–04 and 2002–06, where the return for multi-country funds and the Europe All Vehicles total are also showed. The next most profitable countries are the Netherlands and Italy.

The annual return classified by sector and country of destination for the funds in the period 2004–06 appears in Table 4.8. A fund is referred to as investing in a particular category of real estate when more than 75 per cent of its assets are invested in that category; otherwise it is referred as a diversified fund. The diversified funds offering the highest returns are those that invested in Norway and France, which

Table 4.7   Single- and multi-country fund returns, 2002–6 (annual geometric average, 3-year and 5-year periods; percentages)

	2002–04	**2002–06**
United Kingdom	20.6	16.9
Netherlands	12	11.9
Europe All Vehicles	10	8.9
Italy	8.3	8
Portugal	5.6	7.7
Multi-country	5.7	6.8
Spain	6	6.6
Switzerland	6.2	5.8

Note: Spain is not included in Europe All Vehicles.
Sources: IPD *INREV Index* (January 2008); and INVERCO for Spanish data.

in 2006 offered an annual return of 29.4 per cent and 26.1 per cent, respectively. The only data for the industrial and logistics sector are for the United Kingdom and the multi-country funds, which in 2006 had annual returns of 21.5 per cent and 14.9 per cent, respectively.

Direct and indirect real estate investment

Performance compared

In all the European countries with available data, the investment in listed real estate companies dominated those of real estate funds and direct investment in real estate assets in the 3-year and 5-year periods to 2006; see Table 4.9. The second most profitable option varies from country to country: investment in real estate funds is the second best in the United Kingdom, the Netherlands and Switzerland, whereas direct investment is more profitable than funds in Spain, Italy and Portugal.

While we have the performance of quoted companies in 2007 presented as quite considerable drops in the indices shown earlier (see Figure 4.5), this is not the case with funds and direct investment. As the performance of the latter two is assumed not to be as negative as stocks in 2007, the order of returns mentioned in the previous paragraph would change at some point.

Over the whole of Europe, the highest returns at both 3-year and 5-year are also for investment in listed real estate companies, particularly in the latest three years available (38.7 per cent). Direct investment provides slightly better returns than funds.

Table 4.8   Fund performance by sector and country of investment, various years (annual return in percentages and local currencies)

		Diversified	Industrial/ Logistic	Offices	Residential	Retail
France	2006	26.1				
Germany	2006	4.4				
Italy	2004	9.4				
	2005	7.6				
	2006	11.7				
Norway	2006	29.4				
Netherlands	2004			1.9	11.0	11.1
	2005			8.1	13.7	14.2
	2006			12.6	14.0	18.4
Portugal	2004	7.2				
	2005	6.0				
	2006	3.4				
Switzerland	2004	5.6			5.3	
	2005	5.9				
	2006	8.8				
United Kingdom	2004	16.6	23.2	8.9		28.4
	2005	19.5	17.2	25.4		26.6
	2006	21.1	21.5	30.4		20.4
Multi-country	2004	4.2	14.3	−5.9		23.6
	2005	2.9	30.1	21.0		27.2
	2006	6.3	14.9	15.7		20.4

Note: Based on 206 European funds, 128 at national level and 78 multi-country funds. The INREV indices were unfrozen indices at the time of going to print and therefore subject to change.
Source: IPD *INREV Index* (January 2008).

In the USA, the returns on listed companies (REITs) are also larger than those on direct investment. Over the 3-year and 5-year periods, stocks performed better in Europe, while direct investment was preferable in USA in both periods.

Beyond performance

There are more criteria than merely returns to examine in the different categories of indirect investment; some of those that are more relevant to potential investors are as follows. The alleged advantages and

Table 4.9 Performance of real estate companies, funds and direct investment, 3-year and 5-year periods, 2002–06 (geometric averaged annual return in local currencies; percentages)

Country	Real estate companies		Real estate funds		Direct Investment in real estate	
	3 yrs 2002–04	5 yrs 2002–06	3 yrs 2002–04	5 yrs 2002–06	3 yrs 2002–04	5 yrs 2002–06
United Kingdom	37.1	27.6	20.6	16.9	18.5	15.1
The Netherlands	32.3	25.9	12.0	11.9	10.2	9.3
France	47.6	35.9	–	–	14	11.4
Spain	49.6	43.3	6.0	6.6	15.3	12.4
Germany	39.6	15.8	–	–	1.0	1.9
Sweden	41.5	31.4	–	–	11.5	7.4
Switzerland	21.1	14.7	6.2	5.8	5.4	5.4
Italy	46.4	28.3	8.3	8.0	8.4	9.0
Portugal			5.6	7.7	11	11.3
Europe	38.7	26.9	10.0	8.9	11.5	9.7
	REITs		Real estate funds		Direct Investment	
USA	27.2	23.5	–	–	17.0	13.2

Note: The 5-year period return for the direct investment in Italy corresponds in fact to a 4-year period. The real estate investment fund returns are influenced by portfolio composition.
Sources: IPD *INREV Index* (www.inrev.org) (January 2008); Thomson DataStream (accessed June 2008); INVERCO for Spanish real estate funds.

disadvantages of each type of vehicle *vis-à-vis* the other are shown in Table 4.10.

The mandatory dividend payment for REITs is both an advantage, because it means regular payments for shareholders, and a disadvantage, because of the drainage of funds and lower growth potential. The cost of buying or selling REIT shares is very low. Thanks to economies of scale, the cost of debt for investors is significantly reduced. Also, fiscal transparency lessens the tax burden. Investors have the opportunity to participate in the development of the market's most stable companies.

Turning to real estate funds, the advantage for the funds themselves, as with REITs, is that both large and small investors may invest in them, unlike direct investment. Not being listed, they are not subject to variations in stock market prices and so have less exposure to risk. Finally, the fact that they have no obligation to distribute dividends means that they have no problem in remaining fully capitalized.

Table 4.10   Public companies versus investment funds

	Advantages	Disadvantages
REITs	Attract a broad range of investors (both retail and institutional)	Problems of capitalization; grow more slowly because of dividend payments
	More liquidity, stable dividend income	Strict guidelines; these can hamper potentially profitable investment opportunities in other non-real-estate investment markets
	Low commercial transaction costs	Special regulatory status, stock exchange listing, approval by public institutions
	Lower cost of debt; lower tax pressure	Limited leverage and investment activities
	Strict guidelines reduce investor risk	Vulnerability to stock market volatility
	Some of the most stable companies on the market	
Funds	Mainly focused to either retail investors or institutionals	Limitations on investment in other sectors and restricted activities
	Less exposure to risk (in core funds)	No tax transparency in most circumstances
	Capitalization of the fund	Lack of information and transparency
	Access to specialist sectors and new markets	Lack of liquidity
	Access to gearing for institutional investors	No valuation and benchmarking technique High management fees

The disadvantages are the legal restrictions on investment in other sectors, the constraints on certain activities, the obligation to diversify the fund's portfolio risk by maintaining mandatory investment percentages, and the lack of fiscal transparency – mainly in closed-ended funds. With real estate funds there is sometimes a lack of information and transparency. And, not being listed, there is no imposed valuation or benchmarking technique. They also lack liquidity, as selling shares in a fund is very complicated. Finally, management fees can be quite high.

Appendix: Insurance Companies' and Pension Funds' Investment in Real Estate in Europe

Note: This Appendix is based on an updated version of Suárez and Hernández (2006).

Total investment by insurance companies in Europe at the end of 2005, according to the *Comité Européen des Assurances* (CEA), was 6.3 trillion euros, of which 273.4 billion euros were invested in real estate. See Table 4.11, which includes the countries with data available among the CEA member countries that have taken part in the study. The countries with the highest level of investment were the United Kingdom, France and Germany. Among the countries studied, the Central and Eastern European countries are, generally speaking, those with the lowest investment volumes in real estate. The total investment for the Euro Zone is 124.1 billion euros.

Fixed-income securities are the instrument most commonly used for European investments, with France being the country where the highest proportion is allocated to this investment category in absolute and relative terms; see Table 4.12. In the Republic of Ireland, the United Kingdom and Sweden, variable-yield securities are the predominant investment, and they are also the only European countries where this category comprises more than 40 per cent of the total invested. Germany is the only country in which loans are the predominant investment; the weight of this category is substantially lower in the other countries.

During the period 1997–2005, the weight of investment in real estate by insurance companies has decreased, as can be seen from Figure 4.15. The evolution of the weight of the investment in shares indicates the evolution of their value, not necessarily their purchases and sales. Observing the individual evolution of certain countries, it can be seen, for example, that investment in real estate fell in 1999–2000 simply because the value of the investment in shares increased. The opposite effect is seen for subsequent years.

In spite of the decreased weight of real estate in the total investment in recent years, the volume of investment in real estate has grown, only at a much slower rate than the other asset categories; see Figure 4.16. Investment in real estate grew by 22 per cent during the period 1999–2005. The highest growth was in shares and fixed-income securities (196 per cent and 179 per cent, respectively).

The data on real estate investment shown above refers to direct investment and does not include indirect investment in real estate companies and investment funds, nor investments in mortgage loans, or mortgage-related securities, such as mortgage bonds, MBS and others.

Table 4.11 Insurance companies' investment, by categories (in millions of euros) 2005

Ranking by insurace premium	Country	Debt securities and other fixed-income securities	Shares and other variable-yield securities and units in unit trusts	Loans, including loans guaranteed by mortgages	Investments in affiliated undertakings and participating interests	Land and buildings and participating interests	Deposits with credit institutions and other investments	Total
1	United Kingdom	299,757	814,452		285,249	113,576	142,165	1,655,199
2	France	839,163	358,253	13,567		50,918	15,778	1,277,679
3	Germany	123,588	283,001	574,434	131,665	24,251	18,716	1,155,655
4	Italy	230,847	38,354	1,927	26,406	5,770	156,160	459,464
5	Netherlands	130,476	93,649	40,629	10,178	13,202	36,795	324,929
6	Spain	98,374	10,347	1,470	16,553	5,068	41,511	173,323
7	Switzerland	135,895	21,527	23,929	35,988	22,621	32,382	272,342
8	Belgium	114,704	41,606	6,052	11,285	3,870	6,280	183,797
9	Sweden	118,501	131,197	1,693	18,692	7,795	10,710	288,588
10	Denmark	102,898	41,666		24,107	4,459	10,419	183,549
11	Austria	23,570	21,431	5,758	7,843	3,290	3,876	65,768
12	Finland	52,924	34,550	2,798	785	9,439	850	101,346
13	Rep. of Ireland	18,690	46,117			5,810	8,273	78,890
14	Portugal	22,210	4,227	67	729	1,183	11,785	40,201
18	Turkey	3,113	38		1,258	394	1,430	6,233
19	Greece	3,729	1,391		510	967	2,670	9,267
21	Czech Republic	5,611	1,101	156		306	1,816	8,990
23	Slovenia	1,483	1,317	21	176	159	615	3,771
24	Slovakia	1,197	19	225	297	79	353	2,170
27	Cyprus	550	440	113	21	142	488	1,754
29	Lithuania		2		2	33	385	422
31	Latvia	75	14	7	5	17	64	182
32	Malta	570	240		30	63	331	1,234
33	Estonia	205	71	2	11	1	39	329
	Euro Zone	1,660,878	934,923	646,836	206,181	124,132	304,128	3,877,078
	Total	2,328,130	1,945,010	672,848	57,179	273,413	503,891	6,295,082

Table 4.12 Insurance companies' investment, by categories, proportion of each class in total investment

Ranking by insurace premium	Country	Debt securities and other fixed-income securities (%)	Shares and other variable-yield securities and units in unit trusts (%)	Loans, including loans guaranteed by mortgages (%)	Investments in affiliated undertakings and participating interests (%)	Land and buildings and participating interests (%)	Deposits with credit institutions and other investments (%)
1	United Kingdom	18.1	49.2	17.2	6.9	8.6	
2	France	65.7	28.0	1.1	4.0	1.2	1.6
3	Germany	10.7	24.5	49.7	11.4	2.1	34.0
4	Italy	50.2	8.3	0.4	5.7	1.3	11.3
5	Netherlands	40.2	28.8	12.5	3.1	4.1	24.0
6	Spain	56.8	6.0	0.8	9.6	2.9	11.9
7	Switzerland	49.9	7.9	8.8	13.2	8.3	3.4
8	Belgium	62.4	22.6	3.3	6.1	2.1	3.7
9	Sweden	41.1	45.5	0.6	6.5	2.7	
10	Denmark	56.1	22.7	13.1	2.4	5.7	
11	Austria	35.8	32.6	8.8	11.9	5.0	5.9
12	Finland	52.2	34.1	2.8	0.8	9.3	0.8
13	Rep. of Ireland	23.7	58.5	7.4	10.5		
14	Portugal	55.2	10.5	0.2	1.8	2.9	29.3
18	Turkey	49.9	0.6	20.2	6.3	22.9	
19	Greece	40.2	15.0	5.5	10.4	28.8	
21	Czech Republic	62.4	12.2	1.7	3.4	20.2	
23	Slovenia	39.3	34.9	0.6	4.7	4.2	16.3
24	Slovakia	55.2	0.9	10.4	13.7	3.6	16.3
27	Cyprus	31.4	25.1	6.4	1.2	8.1	27.8
29	Lithuania	0.5	0.5	7.8	91.2		35.2
31	Latvia	41.2	7.7	3.8	2.7	9.3	
32	Malta	46.2	19.4	2.4	5.1	26.8	
33	Estonia	62.3	21.6	0.6	3.3	0.3	11.9
	Euro Zone	42.8	24.1	16.7	5.3	3.2	7.8
	Total	37.0	30.9	10.7	9.1	4.3	8.0

Source: CEA (2007).

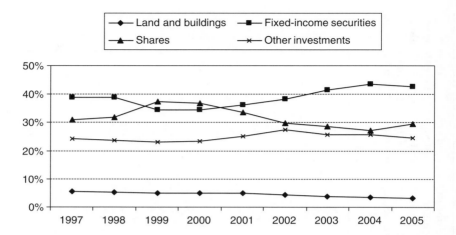

Figure 4.15 Insurance companies' investment by category, 1997–2005 (weight of each category out of the total investment)
Source: CEA *European Insurance in Figures* (2006).

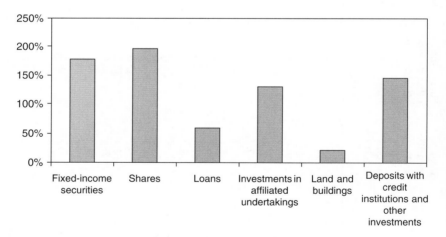

Figure 4.16 Variation of insurance companies' investments by category, EU-12, 1999–2005 (percentages)
Source: CEA *European Insurance in Figures* (2006).

Table 4.13 Real estate portfolio of insurance companies and pension funds, Germany, 2005

Investment in real estate	Percentage of total investment portfolio
Direct	2.0
Indirect. Mainly shares in property companies and funds	3.0
Direct plus indirect	5.0
Loans guaranteed by mortgages and other loans	6.3
Total investment in real estate	11.3

Sources: GDV (Gesamtverband der Deutschen Versicherungswirtschaft e.V.); and Federal Financial Supervisory Authority (2007).

This is because this data is not available at aggregate level and is often not even available in the companies' Annual Reports. There are only isolated pieces of information, such as that, in the Netherlands, 8.5 per cent of life investments and 1.2 per cent of non-life investments are represented by mortgages.

It is possible to offer a greater breakdown of the German insurance companies' investment in real estate. The Investment Ordinance in Germany, which came into force on 1 January 2002, allows more possibilities for investing in real estate assets, such as investment companies, funds or certificates, which would come into the category of *asset-backed securities*. Although investments in real estate only account for 2 per cent of total investments, if the indirect investments (mainly foreign), property funds or investments in property companies were included, they would represent 5 per cent of the total; see Table 4.13.

The weight of the investment in real estate out of the total investment by *pension funds* varies across the European Union countries; see Table 4.14. In 1994, the countries whose pension funds placed the largest proportion of their investments in real estate were Italy (23 per cent), the Netherlands (13 per cent), Finland (12 per cent) and Germany (11 per cent). On the other hand, the countries that invested the least are Greece (nil), Spain (1 per cent), Austria (2 per cent), and Portugal (3 per cent).

Table 4.14   European pension funds' investment by category, 1994

Country	Shares (%)	Fixed-income securities (%)	Land and buildings (%)	Deposits with credit institutions (%)
United Kingdom	77	14	5	4
Netherlands	29	56	13	2
Germany	11	75	11	3
Sweden	32	47	8	12
France	14	39	7	40
Denmark	22	65	9	4
Italy	9	62	23	6
Rep. of Ireland	55	35	6	4
Spain	4	82	1	13
Finland	5	73	12	10
Belgium	36	47	7	10
Portugal	10	72	3	15
Austria	11	75	2	12
Luxembourg	20	70	0	10

Source: ICEA *Las inversiones de los Fondos de Pensiones en la UE.*

References

ABN-AMRO/IPD (2003) *Directory of European Property Vehicles*.

CEA (Comité des Enterprises d'Assurance) (2007) *European Insurance in Figures*, Statistics No. 31 (August).

EPRA (European Public Real Estate Association) (2007) *EPRA Global REIT Survey: A Comparison of the Major REIT Regimes in the World* (August).

Europe Real Estate (2007) *Europe Real Estate Yearbook*.

GDV (Gesamtverband der Deutschen Versicherungswirtschaft e.V.) and Federal Financial Supervisory Authority (2007) *Statistical Yearbook on German Insurance 2007*.

INREV (Investment in Non-listed Real Estate Vehicles).

INREV (2007) *European Non-listed Real Estate Vehicles*, Quarterly Research Report, No. 14 (February).

Investigación Cooperativa entre Compañías Aseguradoras y Fondos de Pensiones (ICEA), *Las inversiones de los Fondos de Pensiones en la UE.*

Investment Property Databank (IPD).

IPD (2008) *INREV Index* (January).

IXIS AEW Europe, Research and Strategy, *The German Open-ended Fund Market – Stressed?*

Maurer, R., Frank R. and Rogalla, R. (2004) 'Return and Risk of German Open-ended Real Estate Funds', *Journal of Property Research* (September).

Piserra, J. (2005) 'Fondos alemanes a la baja', *Expansión Inmobiliario* (21 April): 54.

Suárez J. L. and Vassallo, A. (2005) 'Indirect Investment in Real Estate: Listed Companies and Funds', *IESE Business School Research Paper DI-602* (July).

Suárez J. L. and Hernández, R. (2006) 'Políticas de Inversión del Sector Seguros y de Pensiones en la Unión Europea. Inversión en Inmuebles', Research Paper DI662, IESE Business School, (December).

www.reitnet.com

5
Real Estate Financing: Residential Mortgage Markets

In many ways, the main characteristic of European mortgage markets at the time of writing is their diversity in regulation, product types and lenders. Although they have points in common, each national market works differently, and this makes it difficult to integrate them.*

Residential mortgage credit outstanding in the EU-27 increased from approximately 2.5 trillion euros in 1997 to 5.7 trillions in 2006 (European Mortgage Federation, 2007). The increase is a result of the trend in prices, especially house prices, which have risen in all European countries apart from Germany and Austria (see Chapter 1 regarding recent housing developments in Europe); the large drop in interest rates to historic low levels before 2006; and, in some European countries, tax advantages and an increase in disposable income. However, there were signs of deceleration in the rate of growth of mortgage lending in 2007, and a clear-cut diminution in some countries in 2008.

In the Euro Zone, the ratio of residential mortgages to total loans, which was 39 per cent in 1995, increased to 70.8 per cent in 2006, again reflecting the growing importance of the mortgage market in the financial system. European credit institutions have created innovative products, including self-certified products, interest-only mortgages, mortgage loans that can be used as consumer loans, loans linked to pension funds, or flexible mortgages that can be adapted to uncertain income flows ('la Caixa' Research Department, *El crecimiento del mercado hipotecario europeo*).

The growth of the mortgage market also contributed to the rise in household indebtedness in Europe; between December 2003 and August

---

* This chapter includes concepts and data from Suárez and Vassallo, 2004.

2006 the level of household indebtedness rose by 25.8 per cent – more than the rise in the entire decade 1991–2001 (20 per cent), and mortgage loans become the principal household debt. The loans granted to EMU householders by credit institutions in December 2006 were 70.8 per cent for home-buying, 13 per cent for purchases on credit, and 16.3 per cent for other purposes.

Despite this development, cross-border lending between European countries is still very low. This fact, and the growing importance of mortgage credit, is one of the reasons why efforts are being made to lay the foundations for European integration which, it is hoped, will further stimulate market development. Recent initiatives in that direction at the European level include the European Code of Conduct, signed in 2001, pursuing the standardization of consumer information; and the study commissioned by the European Mortgage Federation and prepared by Mercer Oliver Wyman, entitled *Study on the Financial Integration of European Mortgage Markets*, which identifies barriers to mortgage integration and explores solutions to achieve the benefits of integration. More recently, the European Commission has published a White Paper on Mortgage Markets, which addresses the areas and forms of regulation required to achieve the goal of integrating the European mortgage market. Implementation of the recommendations contained in this White Paper should begin in 2008, but there are doubts as to whether regulation is the best way to achieve integration.

It is hoped that the benefits of increased integration in mortgage markets will result in greater choice and cheaper mortgages for borrowers, as well as lower funding and risk-management costs for lenders.

Description of the European mortgage markets

As was stated earlier, the main feature of the mortgage market in Europe is its fragmentation. Across countries, there is a great variety of products, prices and customers, as well as variations in the types of contracts available and the operating institutions. The characteristics of contracts and institutions are the result of historical differences in demographics and political and regulatory frameworks, as well as in consumer preferences. Types of loans differ, referring, among other characteristics, to the loan-to-value ratio, the duration of the loan, and the adjustment of the interest rate over the life of the loan. In each country, mortgage loans may include financial and non-financial services. These are additional services related to the mortgage, such as associated insurance products.

The increase in the proportion of mortgages in relation to total bank lending has led to fiercer competition among financial institutions to maintain or expand their market share. As far as the lenders are concerned, according to data published by the European Mortgage Federation, in some countries (such as Italy and Portugal) the mortgage market is dominated by *universal banks*, and in others by *commercial banks*, notably in Belgium, Greece, the Republic of Ireland, and Finland. In Spain, Germany and Austria an important role is played by *savings banks*, representing a significant share of the mortgage market. In Denmark and Sweden, by contrast, *mortgage credit institutions* control a large part of the market. Co-operative and mutual institutions are major players in some countries (such as the *Bausparkassen* in Germany, and similar institutions in Austria and Finland), and the *building societies* in the Republic of Ireland and the United Kingdom. Finally, *insurance companies* and *pension funds* are active participants in the mortgage market in Austria, the Netherlands, Germany, Finland and Belgium.

Mortgage market volume

Since the late 1990s, the balance of mortgage loans outstanding has increased in all European countries, basically because in most countries there has been a growing tendency for people to buy their own homes. This trend has been encouraged by fiscal policies that favour home buying over home rental (as, for example, in countries such as the Netherlands and Portugal); by enhanced income expectations (in countries such as the Netherlands, Portugal and Spain); and the reduction of interest rates, reaching low historical levels for most countries before December 2005. Other factors that favoured such growth were increased loan-to-value ratio, which at times exceeded 100 per cent; increased time to pay (35 years is now not unusual in some countries); and innovation in mortgage product offerings, such as 'made-to-measure' mortgages to suit the circumstances of the consumer; or 'payment holidays', where repayments may be deferred if the borrower experiences a period of financial difficulty.

There is a fairly wide range of sizes among the national markets in the EU-27; from the enormous markets of the United Kingdom and Germany, to the tiny markets of most new member states. The country with the largest residential mortgage balance outstanding in 2006 was the United Kingdom, followed by Germany, France and Spain. Before 2004, Germany had always occupied first place, but the maturity of its market has meant that only small, incremental gains were possible in the last few years. The Netherlands was in fifth place, with a total of 525 billion euros; see Table 5.1.

Table 5.1 Residential mortgage balances outstanding, Europe, 2006 (in millions of euros and percentages)

	Outstanding balance 2006	Growth (%)	
		2005–06	1997–2006
United Kingdom	1,583,372	11.9	144.8
Germany	1,183,834	1.8	25.6
France	577,800	14.7	127.5
Spain	571,746	20.2	448.2
Netherlands	525,874	7.9	212.7
Italy	276,102	13.3	267.5
Denmark	221,970	13.4	108.7
Sweden	173,499	9.1	61.2
Republic of Ireland	123,288	24.6	617
Belgium	114,105	16.4	107.2
Portugal	91,895	15.7	117.9
Finland	73,200	11.0	129.3
Austria	60,669	12.7	104.7
Greece	57,145	25.8	912.1
Poland	22,514	53.7	1,005.3
Luxembourg	11,345	13.4	213.8
Hungary	10,215	11.0	710.1
Czech Republic	8,055	33.9	426.1
Latvia	4,680	86.5	9,650
Estonia	4,278	63.4	2,212.4
Slovakia	4,209	36.7	316.3
Cyprus	3,077	43.5	899
Lithuania	2,997	32.1	3,344.8
Romania	2,276	57.1	147.1
Slovenia	1,956	50.3	3,661.5
Malta	1,770	16.5	506.2
Bulgaria	1,745	73.5	3,958.1
EU-27	5,713,616	11.1	119.9
Switzerland	307,348	3.4	72.8
Turkey	12,237	65.7	1,876.9
Croatia	5,219	37.2	436.4
Ukraine	4,301	157.5	6,416.7
Serbia	650	111.7	16,150

Note: For many countries, especially the new member states of the EU-27, there is no data available for 1996. Instead, we have used data from 1998 for Estonia, Cyprus and Lithuania; 1999 for Latvia, Slovenia, Malta, Bulgaria and Portugal; 2001 for Austria; 2002 for the Czech Republic and Slovakia; and 2004 for Romania.
Source: European Mortgage Federation (2007).

In many countries there has been a marked growth in lending. Over the period 1997–2006, the volume of residential mortgage loans outstanding in Europe doubled, to reach 5.7 trillion euros, having grown at an average rate of 12 per cent per year, representing 49.4 per cent of the combined GDP of all European countries. The growth in that period has been most significant in the new member states of the EU-27, as can be seen from figures such as 9,650 per cent in Latvia and 3,958 per cent in Bulgaria; enormous figures by any measure, but especially when compared to Germany or Sweden, with 25.6 per cent and 61.2 per cent, respectively. Long-term loans in Slovenia only account for 20 per cent of the total existing loans.

New EU member states are experiencing a fairly brisk level of construction; thanks in part to low interest rates, but also to increasing bank competition, which has seen the bank profit margins, and therefore the cost of credit, being reduced significantly. This, in turn, is leading to greater access to credit for many families, and strong lending activity. Accordingly, these new member states of the EU-27 showed a remarkable growth in the residential loan market during the year 2005–6; see Figure 5.1.

Mortgage lending increased in all the EU countries, despite the fact that those countries with mature mortgage markets, such as Germany,

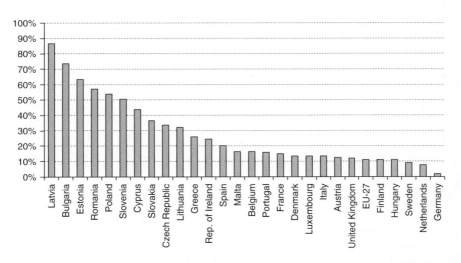

Figure 5.1 Growth of residential mortgage loans outstanding, EU-27, 2005–6 (percentages)
Source: European Mortgage Federation (2007).

the Netherlands and the United Kingdom, have clearly experienced a slowdown. The modest growth in Germany (1.8 per cent) and the Netherlands (7.9 per cent) pales in comparison with new member states; Latvia (86.5 per cent), Bulgaria (73.5 per cent), Estonia (63.4 per cent), Romania (57.1 per cent), Poland (53.7 per cent), Slovenia (50.3 per cent), Cyprus (43.5 per cent) and Slovakia (36.7 per cent). The mortgage market of Hungary, also a new member country, has grown more slowly than the other new members because of the removal of state subsidies after 2003.

Among the older members of the EU, the countries with the greatest growth in 2006 were Greece, with a growth of 25.8 per cent, and the

Table 5.2   Gross residential mortgage loans, selected EU-27 countries, Croatia and Turkey, 2006 (in millions of euros)

	Gross residential loans 2006	Growth (%)	
		2005–06	1997–2006
EU-27 countries with available data			
Estonia	2,339	59	
Czech Republic	4,094	57	
Lithuania	1,171	35	
Hungary	2,611	35	
United Kingdom	505,928	20	337
Republic of Ireland	39,872	17	1,011
Greece	15,444	13	
Italy	89,657	13	327
Spain	155,676	12	431
France	149,080	11	218
Luxembourg	4,376	11	246
Netherlands	119,000	4	146
Germany	107,000	4	
Belgium	24,328	−3	82
Sweden	41,289	−6	116
Finland	27,000	−6	310
Denmark	56,171	−35	127
Total	**1,253,751**		
Other countries			
Croatia	1,378	60	
Turkey	8,626	24	

Source: European Mortgage Federation (2007).

Republic of Ireland, with 24.6 per cent. The growth in Greece was mainly as a result of changes in the methodology of property valuation, which brought several fiscal advantages. Spain also experienced important growth in this market, with outstanding residential mortgages totalling 572 billion euros at the end of 2006.

Lending activity

The growth in the number and volume of mortgages granted (gross mortgage lending) compared to the mortgages either paid off or cancelled, leads to a net positive sum that fuels the increase in the mortgage outstanding balance. Gross new residential mortgage lending in 2006 amounted to 1.2 trillion euros for the countries with available data – more than four times the amount in 1996; see Table 5.2.

The growth of gross lending across countries is similar to the increase in outstanding balances; countries with a high growth rate of lending tend to have high level of mortgage outstanding. The period studied presents a relevant expansion in the mortgage market; see Figure 5.2.

In mid-2007, financial turmoil was unleashed, triggered by the subprime sector of the US mortgage market that spread its effects over the

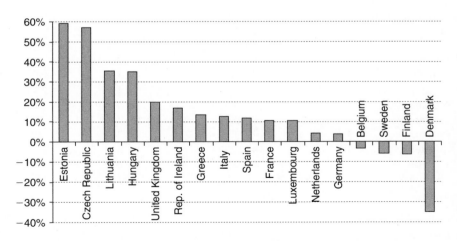

Figure 5.2 Growth of gross residential mortgage loans, selected European countries, 2005–6
Source: European Mortgage Federation (2007).

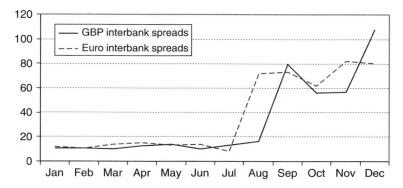

Figure 5.3 3-month interbank spreads, 2007 (interbank rate minus treasury bills rates; basis points; pounds sterling and euros)
Sources: Bank of England; Bank of Spain.

different segments of lending activity. At the time of writing, the financial institutions are showing signs of a lack of liquidity amid a certain degree of mutual distrust that is putting pressure on the interbank markets. In that sense, the most evident symptom of the lack of liquidity is the increase in interbank rates; see Figure 5.3.

Low intermediary liquidity added to the reduced activity in certain housing markets in 2007, thus reducing mortgage lending demand and supply in many countries. The gross lending figures in some countries reduced their rate of growth in 2007, and in certain countries they fell, as indicated by the data available so far. See Figure 5.4 for the monthly gross lending volume in 2007 for the United Kingdom and Spain. In the latter country, the lending volume from January to November 2007 decreased by 4.5 per cent from the previous year. In the United Kingdom, the annual lending volume in 2007 was 6.9 per cent lower than in 2006, with the final months of the year decreasing the most.

Despite the fact that the individual country markets are quite separate and unrelated to one another, it is worth noting that foreign currency mortgage lending has been growing significantly in recent years, mainly in the Central and Eastern European regions. In certain countries in the CEE, the most popular foreign currencies are the euro and the Swiss franc. Borrowers are attracted by the low interest rates in foreign currency and the financial institutions by the high spreads applied and the low default rate see Figure 5.5.

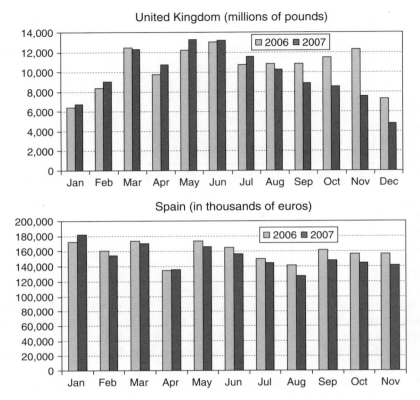

United Kingdom (millions of pounds)

Spain (in thousands of euros)

Figure 5.4 Monthly gross lending, United Kingdom and Spain, 2006–7 (millions of pounds and thousands of euros)
Sources: Bank of England (Statistical Interactive Database) and Instituto National de Estadistica (INE) (both accessed February 2008).

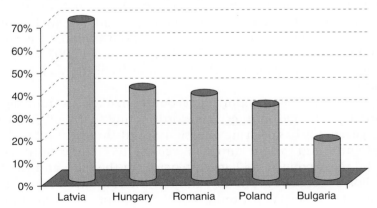

Figure 5.5 Mortgage loans in foreign currency, selected CEE countries, June 2006 (mortgage loans in foreign currency to overall lending ratio)
Sources: European Mortgage Federation (2007), National Central Banks and PNB Paribas.

Mortgage origination in the USA has been recording negative variation rates since the second quarter of 2006, and with two-digit
negative rates since the third quarter; see Figure 5.6.

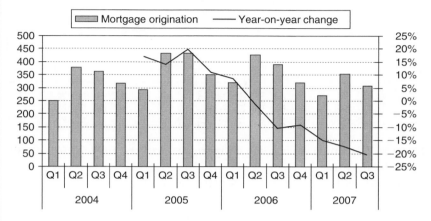

Figure 5.6   US mortgage origination for house purchase purposes, 2004–7
(in billions of US dollars)
Source: Mortgage Bankers Association.

The reduction in new mortgage loans in the USA was caused by
the cooling of the housing market (discussed in Chapter 1) and the
financial squeeze that began in 2007, triggered by the subprime mortgages crisis. As noted in Chapter 1, subprime loans are loans granted
to people who lack a reliable credit track record, creating a high-yield,
high-risk asset for financial institutions. The delinquency rate of subprime mortgages has risen sharply in recent years, and at the time of
writing is at an all-time high; see Figure 5.7.

The weight of subprime loans in the total of mortgage loans outstanding was 13 per cent as at the end of the second quarter of 2007.
While the vast majority of prime mortgages are based on fixed interest rates, most of the subprime mortgages have variable rates, and
these are the mortgages with the higher default rate. This has forced
the US government to bring in emergency measures to help people
with these loans. Serious delinquency rates on subprime mortgages
are ten times higher than those on prime conventional mortgages,
and are likely to exceed their previous high in 2002. Declining
home values and stagnant home sales markets prevent many borrowers from selling their homes or from refinancing themselves out
of trouble.

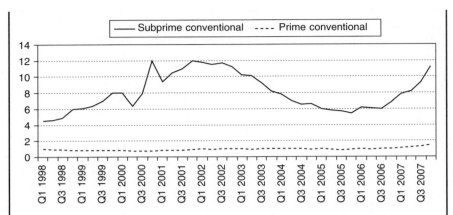

Figure 5.7   Delinquency rates in US mortgage markets, 1998–2007 (percentage of total loans)

Source: Mortgage Bankers Association National Delinquency Survey.

Although the subprime crisis has affected many financial institutions, and some second-order institutions have even defaulted, the biggest problems have arisen in the secondary markets, where these loans have been securitized and embedded in second- or third-order financial instruments that have been devalued, as will be seen in Chapter 6. As of January 2008, the total knock-on effect of this situation to date has caused top-level global financial institutions to write down about 120 billion dollars of loans.

Mortgage markets and the economy

The ratio of outstanding balance to GDP in the EU-27 allows us to rank the relative contribution of mortgage markets to each economy, as well as demonstrating the high level of indebtedness experienced in recent years, rising from 32 per cent in 1996 to 49.4 per cent in 2006. This ratio has grown in all the EU-27 countries, apart from Germany in the past few years, as the growth in the mortgage market has been greater than the growth in GDP. In 2006, the GDP growth in the EU-27 was 3 per cent, and the corresponding increase in mortgages outstanding was 11.1 per cent, as was shown in Table 5.1.

Those countries in the lead with mortgages outstanding relative to GDP are Denmark, the Netherlands and the United Kingdom, where the mortgage markets are well-established and seem set to continue, since this development has provided families with easier access to credit. The

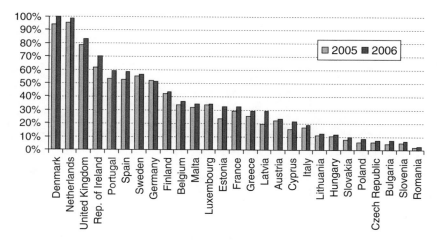

Figure 5.8 Residential mortgage loans outstanding in relation to GDP, EU-27, 2005 and 2006 (Residential mortgage loans outstanding/GDP; percentages)
Source: European Mortgage Federation (2007).

growth in this ratio in 2006 in the Netherlands has been significant, a result of the generous interest rate relief available (although the state wishes to reduce it); see Figure 5.8.

Following the United Kingdom, we find the Republic of Ireland, Portugal, Spain and Sweden. The Republic of Ireland, Portugal and Spain had low mortgage-to-GDP ratios in 1996 but, as a consequence of financial deregulation and the creation of innovative products, all showed strong performance a decade later.

Another measure of the importance of the mortgage markets is the size of these products relative to the total loans offered by financial institutions. Without doubt, mortgages play a key role in the activities of financial institutions, as is demonstrated by the level of mortgages as a proportion of the total loans they offer, as shown in Figure 5.9.

The ratio increased in all the countries after 1996, apart from Germany, which remained fairly stable until 2006, reflecting the maturity of its mortgage market (similar to that of the United Kingdom, where the ratio has increased slowly) and the efforts of the banks to increase their activity in other credit-related areas. Note that Figure 5.9 includes only residential mortgage loans, as the ratio of the mortgage market to total loans would be even higher if we included commercial mortgage loans.

Another measure of the level of mortgage indebtedness is the outstanding balance per capita. The contribution of this measure can be tested with Luxembourg, which appears to be very small when

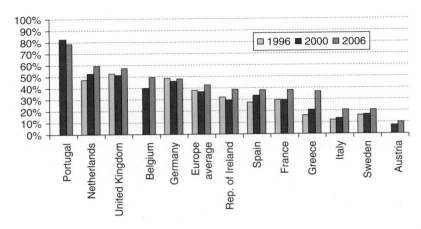

Figure 5.9 Residential mortgage loans/total loans: outstanding balances, selected European countries, 1996, 2000 and 2006 (percentages)
Note: Austria's data are for 2001 and 2006.
Source: European Mortgage Federation (2007), Thomson DataStream (accessed June 2008).

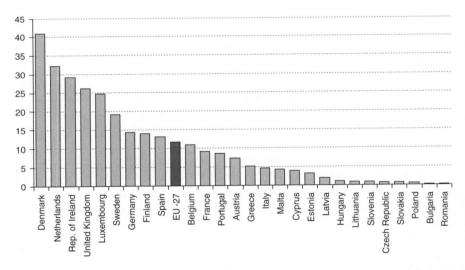

Figure 5.10 Mortgage loans outstanding per capita, EU-27 countries and EU-27 total, 2006 (000s euros)
Source: European Mortgage Federation (2007).

considering the absolute numbers of the market, but in actual fact it now turns out to be fifth in the EU. On the other hand, France or Italy rank third and sixth in the EU in absolute terms, but in per capita terms both are below the average, as shown in Figure 5.10.

The countries above the EU-27 average of 11,600 euros per person can be classified into three groups: (i) those with a mature mortgage market and a large number of transaction, such as the United Kingdom, Germany, the Netherlands and Sweden; (ii) those smaller markets in absolute terms that nevertheless have a high level of activity in relative terms, such as Luxembourg and Finland; and (iii) countries such as Denmark, Spain and the Republic of Ireland, whose mortgage activity has been significant in recent years and has reached a considerable level.

All the new EU member states are below the EU average, as also is Greece, with a very significant growth but still in a 'catch-up' phase despite having entered the EU at the same time as Spain and the Republic of Ireland. Italy comes next, with very considerable growth since the mid-1990s. And finally appear countries such as Austria, Portugal, Belgium and France, which have trailed behind since the mid-1990s.

Household indebtedness

Over the period 1997–2006, household indebtedness increased in the EU-27 as a whole as well as in individual countries. In Spain, Portugal and the Republic of Ireland, household indebtedness grew considerably because of the steady development of these countries' financial markets and the boost they received from membership of the European Monetary Union (EMU). Another factor was the rapid increase in mortgage lending. In France, by contrast, the level of indebtedness, which was already below the EMU average, did not increase very much. Austria showed an increase, but still remained well below the EMU average.

The growth of mortgage lending has played an important part in the overall increase in household indebtedness in recent years. In fact, the bulk (70.8 per cent) of bank loans granted to households in the Euro Zone is earmarked for house purchase; see Table 5.3.

The Netherlands is ranked first in borrowing for house purchase, with 88 per cent, followed by Denmark, Estonia, Portugal and the Republic of Ireland. The last three have been among the countries that have seen a notable expansion of their mortgage markets.

Although it might seem somewhat paradoxical, there is not much correlation between household indebtedness and the rate of owner occupancy; see Figure 5.11. Although Austria has a very low level of indebtedness and a similarly low level of owner occupancy, Italy has a low percentage of household indebtedness but a very high level of owner occupancy – much higher than France, for example, which has a higher level of indebtedness. Similarly, the mortgage balance outstanding is also comparatively high in Germany, contributing to high levels

Table 5.3 Household borrowing by destination of proceeds, Europe, 2006 (percentages of total loans)

	Housing	Consumer	Other
Netherlands	88.0	5.8	6.2
Denmark	84.9	6.3	8.8
Estonia	82.4	10.2	7.4
Portugal	79.7	9.9	10.4
Republic of Ireland	79.6	14.3	6.1
Belgium	79.5	6.6	13.9
Latvia	75.8	13.8	10.4
Spain	72.9	12.3	14.8
France	72.0	18.8	9.2
Finland	70.9	13.4	15.7
EMU	**70.8**	**13.0**	**16.3**
Malta	69.6	9.9	20.5
Czech Republic	69.2	20.4	10.4
Germany	67.8	11.6	20.6
Slovakia	65.9	15.1	19.0
Greece	65.4	31.9	2.7
Lithuania	65.4	16.2	18.5
Sweden	64.6	6.9	28.6
United Kingdom	57.0	11.4	31.6
Italy	56.7	11.6	31.7
Hungary	56.5	36.3	7.2
Austria	53.2	22.0	24.8
Luxembourg	46.5	5.0	48.5
Poland	41.4	32.8	25.8
Cyprus	39.0	20.5	40.5
Bulgaria	37.8	51.9	10.3
Slovenia	36.3	42.5	21.2
Romania	18.7	79.5	1.8

Note: Percentages for each country or EMU may not add up to 100 per cent due to rounding up.
Sources: Thomson DataStream (accessed June 2008) and European Central Bank.

of household indebtedness, although the rate of owner occupancy is among the lowest in Europe.

One specific measure of household indebtedness is that related to home buying in terms of gross disposable income in the EU. Borrowing for housing purposes has increased recently in most countries and, in the Netherlands, Denmark, the Republic of Ireland, the United Kingdom and Sweden, it is considerably higher than household gross disposable income, as was shown in Table 5.4. In 2006, the ratio of

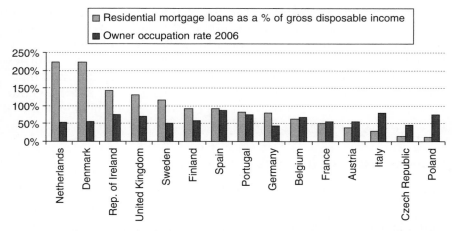

Figure 5.11 Household indebtedness and owner occupancy rate, selected European countries, 2006 (household indebtedness relative to gross disposable income and owner occupancy rate)

Sources: European Mortgage Federation (2007); Thomson DataStream (accessed June 2008).

Table 5.4 Household indebtedness for housing purposes, selected European countries and EMU, 1996, 2000 and 2006 (total outstanding residential loans/gross disposable income of households; percentages)

	1996	2000	2006
Netherlands	86.0	137.1	222.7
Denmark	132.5	174.2	222.4
Republic of Ireland	40.1	59.1	143.1
United Kingdom	86.7	136.8	131.3
Sweden	98.2	92.7	116.1
Finland	61.0	65.3	91.5
Spain	25.5	44.6	91.5
Portugal		59.0	83.3
Germany	73.9	83.0	79.6
EMU		**42.8**	**69.7**
Belgium	37.4	44.8	62.1
France	31.5	34.2	51.4
Austria			38.8
Italy	9.8	15.0	28.3
Czech Republic			14.7
Poland	2.2	3.1	13.0

Sources: Thomson DataStream (accessed June 2008); European Mortgage Federation (2007); European Central Bank (accessed June 2008).

indebtedness was 222.7 per cent in the Netherlands, 222.4 per cent in Denmark, 143.1 per cent in the Republic of Ireland, 131.3 per cent in the United Kingdom, and 116.1 per cent in Sweden, all well above the Euro Zone average of 71 per cent. On the other hand, some countries had a much lower ratio, notably Poland, the Czech Republic and Italy. The ratio of household indebtedness for housing purposes in the Euro Zone increased from 42.8 per cent of gross disposable income in 2000 to 69.7 per cent in 2006.

Characteristics of mortgage loans

Interest rate and terms of mortgages

The terms of mortgage loans vary. On the one hand, in Sweden, the Netherlands, Denmark and Portugal, periods of thirty years are common, whereas in Italy, ten-year mortgages are the norm. In Spain, the average term is around twenty years, though this appears to be increasing with house prices, and thus the size of the sums required.

Fixed-rate mortgages are usual in most European countries, apart from Spain, Portugal, the Republic of Ireland and the United Kingdom. Figure 5.12 shows the types of interest rates for countries with data available. In fact, fixed-rate mortgages represent about two-thirds of the total outstanding. For our purposes, fixed-rate mortgages also include

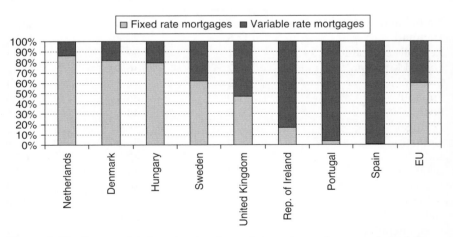

Figure 5.12 Types of interest rate charged, mortgage loans, selected European countries and the EU, 2005 (variable rate mortgages/mortgage lending outstanding)
Source: European Mortgage Federation (2006).

mortgages with only an initial fixed period. The split between fixed and floating interest rates can change in one specific country over time because of changes in relative costs of short-term versus long-term rates, regulations, and the introduction of new products on to the market (European Mortgage Federation, 2006). The differences in the products and the economic context make it difficult to compare interest rate costs among the different European countries. Other costs will be discussed in the next section.

The general decrease in interest rates observed in most countries before 2006 was a crucial factor in the increase of mortgage lending. Low interest rates stimulated borrowing for many households; even more when real interest rates are considered; see Table 5.5.

In fact, five countries had negative real interest rates in 2002: the Republic of Ireland, Spain, Portugal, Greece and the Netherlands; and these were still relatively low in 2006. Also noteworthy is the fact that the most pronounced mortgage expansion was observed in precisely those countries with negative real interest rates in 2002.

It was stated previously that the growth in mortgages outstanding and their proportion to total loans fuelled increased competition among financial institutions. One way of differentiating mortgage products is by differing interest rate charges. A range of mortgage products is shown in the Appendix to this chapter (see page 174).

Table 5.5 Real interbank interest rates, Europe (interest rates minus Consumer Price Index; percentages)

	1992	1997	2002	2006
Belgium	5.66	2.96	1.54	1.81
Finland	8.17	2.48	1.09	2.88
France	8.04	2.79	0.55	2.33
Germany	7.90	2.63	1.55	2.63
Greece		10.09	−0.66	0.65
Republic of Ireland		4.13	−1.85	1.03
Italy		3.38	0.25	1.93
Netherlands	5.16	1.70	−0.45	2.33
Norway			3.11	2.36
Portugal			−1.25	1.53
Spain	8.98	2.68	−1.29	1.16
Sweden	8.29	2.73	2.23	2.35
United Kingdom	4.11	5.89	2.44	2.75

Sources: Thomson DataStream and IMF *World Economic Outlook Database* (both accessed June 2008).

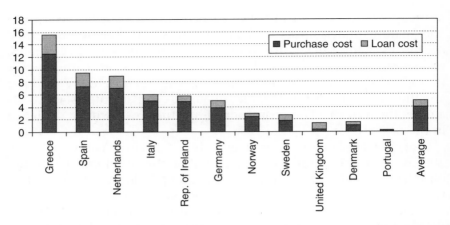

Figure 5.13 Transaction costs across the EU, 2003 (percentage of property purchase price)
Source: Mercer Oliver Wyman (2003).

Mortgage loan costs

Loan costs might include insurance, expert advice, solicitor's and/or notary's services, registration fees, searches, valuations, expenses and fees charged by the lender (not to mention possible extra costs such as brokerage fees, additional or specialized legal expenses and so on). These costs are shown in Figure 5.13. In some European countries, many of the mortgage-related fees are added to the loan, which improves mobility, but the costs are still borne by the borrower (Mercer Oliver Wyman, 2003).

The highest transaction costs are in Greece, Spain and the Netherlands, with a high dispersion from the European average. At the opposite extreme are Portugal, Denmark and the United Kingdom, with very low loan cost. Relatively low transaction costs in the United Kingdom may be a result of it being a highly-developed market with intense competition. In contrast, Denmark and Portugal both have low transaction costs despite the fact that their markets are very concentrated.

Movements towards the European integration of mortgage markets

The first firm step towards integration of the mortgage market came with the enactment of the European Code of Conduct in 2001. This Code was focused primarily on providing transparency and standardized information to borrowers. It has been followed by a series of initiatives aimed at identifying the benefits of increased integration for customers and financial institutions, and specifying the steps that would have to be taken to achieve it and the barriers that might be encountered on the way. It would also be necessary to know the member countries' baseline situation.

This work led to the publication on 19 December 2007 of the White Paper on Mortgage Credit by the European Commission, proposing the subjects requiring a greater degree of regulation, and what form this regulation should take. It should be added that there is no consensus between the different countries as to what regulation is required and how far it should go. Some countries, such as the United Kingdom, advocate a loose regulatory framework and the predominance of self-regulation, but the events that have shaken the mortgage markets in the second half of 2007 have weakened this position. Other tasks that are as yet pending are an analysis of the individual impact of implementing the measures, the inclusion of a thorough cost–benefit analysis, and closing certain legal loopholes. Consequently, the road towards integration of the mortgage market is still far from its destination.

European Code of Conduct

The European Agreement on a Voluntary Code of Conduct for Pre-contractual Information on Home Loans was signed on 5 March 2001 by the European Credit Sector Associations, led by the European Mortgage Federation and consumer organizations. The negotiations as well as the signing of the Agreement were conducted under the aegis of the European Commission. The European Code of Conduct is a step towards the integration of European mortgage markets, its aims being to ensure transparency of information and to facilitate comparison between different markets by means of pre-contractual information to be provided to consumers regarding home loans.

According to the European Mortgage Federation, the object of the Code is to improve and standardize consumer information and help prospective borrowers to choose the mortgage loans best suited to their needs. By standardizing information, the Code is intended to help develop cross-border mortgage transactions and boost competition in the still-fragmented European mortgage markets. The agreement provides backing for a voluntary code of conduct to be implemented by any institution offering home loans to consumers.

Application of the Code throughout Europe has been very successful. By the end of 2007, over 3,800 credit institutions had subscribed to the Code. Table 5.6 shows the number of subscribing institutions in each country, and the percentage they represent of the national total.

Table 5.6 Credit institutions subscribing to the European Code of Conduct

	Number of credit institutions registered	Percentage of the total national mortgage market
Belgium	27	90
Denmark	6	94
Germany	1,454	90
Greece	21	95
France	42	40
Republic of Ireland	12	99
Italy	512	96
Luxembourg	15	90
Netherlands	124	99
Austria	607	99
Portugal	21	95
Finland	334	99
Sweden	90	95
United Kingdom	142	98
Norway	10	40

Source: European Banking Industry Committee (2003, 2005).

Apart from Norway and France, the rate of adoption reached the 90 per cent level or higher. At the time of writing, Spain was the only country that had not yet registered, because of incompatibilities between Spanish legislation and the Code. Since 1994, there has been a 'ministerial order' in Spain requiring transparency of information in mortgage loans and guaranteeing a level of consumer protection equal or superior to that provided by the Code (Mercer Oliver Wyman, 2003).

Other initiatives for European level co-ordination

The way to the integration of mortgage markets has many routes, not all of them within the reach of the EU institutions. Many activities related to mortgage lending are regulated at national level as, for example, valuations, real estate agents, property rights, taxes and subsidies. In some cases the European Union influences mortgage lending indirectly through regulations on bank and consumer solvency.

In March 2003, with the objective of assessing obstacles to the creation of a single credit market in the EU, the Forum Group on Mortgage Credit (Forum Group) was created. It was a step forward in the process of consultation, and proposals for overriding the obstacles were expected.

In November 2003, the European Mortgage Federation (EMF), in collaboration with Mercer Oliver Wyman, carried out a study investigating the state of the mortgage industry and the potential for greater integration. In this joint effort, they identified the benefits to be obtained from greater integration and the barriers to such integration (Mercer Oliver Wyman, 2003). This study offered the state of the art in the European mortgage markets, including a description of the main loan characteristics at a national level, which appears in an Appendix to this chapter.

On 19 July 2005, the European Commission published its Green Paper on Mortgage Credit in the EU. The Green Paper examines the case for Commission action in the EU mortgage credit market. Shortly afterwards, the Commission published the report it had commissioned from *London Economics* on the potential costs and benefits of the further integration of EU Mortgage Markets.

At the beginning of 2006, based on the results of the Mortgage Credit Green Paper consultation, the Commission acknowledged a need for more in-depth analysis, and announced that it would extend its investigation to funding issues and to issues related to consumer protection. To this end, the Commission established its Mortgage Funding Expert Group, and Mortgage Industry and Consumer Dialogue Group. The EMF responded to the Reports of both of these Groups in Position Papers dated 15 January 2007 and 15 February 2007, outlining its position on the outcome of the groups' discussions, and on integration more broadly.

In parallel with the Commission's assessment, the European Parliament decided to deliver an own-initiative report on the Commission's Green Paper on Mortgage Credit. The drafting of the report was divided between the Committee on Economic and Monetary Affairs, which focuses mainly on economic issues, and the Committee on Internal Market and Consumer Protection, which concentrates mainly on consumer-protection-related questions. The Parliament's Legal Committee also delivered an opinion. The Final European Parliament Own Initiative Report, which combined the texts of the three committees, was approved by its Plenary in November 2006.

White Paper on the Integration of EU Mortgage Credit Markets

The European Commission published the White Paper on the Integration of EU Mortgage Credit Markets on 18 December 2007, summarizing the conclusions of a comprehensive review of European residential mortgage markets, and identified a package of proportionate measures designed to enhance the competitiveness and efficiency of EU mortgage markets, which will benefit consumers, mortgage lenders and investors alike. Given the importance of mortgage credit for both EU citizens and the economy at large, an evidence-based approach has been adopted. While recent events in global mortgage markets have confirmed the pertinence of the approach proposed, they have also identified areas where further work needs to be undertaken. The Commission intends to engage speedily with all stakeholders to complete its assessment of the various policy options.

To be effective, any proposed measures must demonstrate that they will create new opportunities for mortgage lenders to access other markets and engage in cross-border activity. They must also show that they will enable a more efficient mortgage-lending process, with economies of scale and scope, which should lower costs. The expected benefits should be balanced against the possible costs of these measures.

The work carried out so far suggests that significant benefits can be expected from further action in several of the areas identified in the White Paper. Many of the measures designed to improve the efficiency and competitiveness of cross-border mortgage lending – on both primary and secondary markets – would also lead to improved product diversity, and potentially to lower prices for consumers. The White Paper identified the importance of accurate information, responsible lending and borrowing, and high quality advice for consumers to ensure that they purchase the best product for their needs. Consumers should also be the beneficiaries of efforts to improve customer mobility through increased transparency and reduced product-tying.

In general terms, investors would face a lower risk when investing in mortgage-backed products, through enhanced market transparency, greater certainty as to the recovery value of their investment, and a broader range of investment opportunities as a result of enhanced product diversity on both primary and secondary markets.

Appendix: Mortgage Products in Europe

The following listing of different countries' mortgage loan types has been compiled from the referred study of Mercer Oliver Wyman (2003), with some data updated with information from www.hypo.org.

Country and range of products

Spain

- Variable-rate (indexed) mortgages, reviewed every 6–12 months, are the most common
- Fixed-rate mortgages are very unusual, only 5 per cent of total
- Innovations:
  - Flexible mortgages
  - Capped rate mortgages.

Germany

Very active market:

- Wide range of highly standardized products
- Efficient funding mechanism: *Pfandbriefe*
- *Bausparkassen*: 10 per cent of mortgage loans
- Adjustable long-term fixed-rate mortgages predominate
- The term of the loans is between 20 and 30 years, with a fixed-rate period of 10 to 15 years
- Variable-rate mortgages are very unusual, only 15 per cent of total
- Indexed variable-rate mortgages are not available, for legal reasons
- Interest-only mortgages, where the borrower pays only interest for a given period(5/10/15 years); repayment is via an insurance policy.

Denmark

- Fixed-rate mortgages denominated in Danish crowns of more than 30 years are the most common
- Variable-rate mortgages denominated in Danish crowns and in euros, with adjustment frequencies between 1 and 10 years; can be considered as loans with constant principal repayments
- Now more 10–30 year variable-rate mortgages are beginning to appear.

Italy

- Mortgages available:
  - Variable-rate (adjustable with respect to a reference index)
  - Fixed-rate
  - Mixed
- Principal repayments may be:
  - Fixed

- ○ Increasing
- ○ Decreasing
- Flexible mortgages
- Interest-only mortgages are also available
- Loan-to-value (LTV) ratio is very low: 50–60 per cent, although Micos Banca is starting to offer mortgages with a LTV of 100 per cent, using mortgage insurance to cover the borrower's additional risk
- High-risk subprime loans are not very common.

Netherlands

- One of the broadest mortgage markets in Europe; furthermore, interest paid on mortgages is not tax-deductible
- Interest-only mortgages with high LTV dominate the market
- Lenders try to offer products tailored to consumer needs; very often, they include mortgages linked to a savings or investment product
- 86 per cent of mortgages are fixed-rate, and of those, 60 per cent are over 10 years.
- 14 per cent of mortgages are variable-rate
- Subprime or self-certified products are not available.

Portugal

- Variable-rate mortgages (not indexed to Euribor) are the most common
- The term tends to be between 20 and 25 years
- Fixed-rate mortgages have always been less popular, although they are becoming more common
- A special feature is subsidized mortgages, which account for a large proportion of mortgage loans outstanding
- High-risk mortgages such as subprime or non-conforming are not available.

United Kingdom

Mortgages differ above all in:

- Repayment structure:
  - ○ Repayment/amortization mortgages
  - ○ Interest-only mortgages
  - ○ Flexible mortgages
- Rate structure:
  - ○ Variable-rate

- o Fixed-rate (very short adjustment periods)
- o Capped-rate
- There are very few long-term fixed-rate products, but there are quite a number of short-term, fixed-rate products aimed at attracting new business
- Innovative, high-risk products:
  - o Offset mortgages (which allow savings and the mortgage to be offset against one another for interest calculations)
  - o Subprime
  - o Buy-to-let
  - o Self-certified loans.

France

- Wide range of products; subsidized mortgages, 0 per cent interest, PEL (*Plan d'épargne logement*), PAP loans (*Prêts pour l'accession à la propriété*), regulated loans
- The most common are fixed-rate
- Variable-rate mortgages account for 30 per cent of total
- Flexible mortgages, interest-only mortgages, capped rate and subprime mortgages are available, but the latter only from specialized lenders.

References

Bank of England (www.bankofengland.co.uk).

Bank of Spain (www.bde.es).

European Banking Industry Committee (EBIC) (2003) *Joint Industry Response to the Consultant's Reports on the Code of Conduct* (November).

European Banking Industry Committee (EBIC) (2005) *Progress Report on the European Code of Conduct on Home Loans* (October).

European Central Bank *Statistical Data Warehouse* (http://sdw.ecb.europa.eu/).

European Mortgage Federation (www.hypo.org).

European Mortgage Federation, *European Code of Conduct.*

European Mortgage Federation (2007) *Hypostat 2006: A Review of Europe's Mortgage and Housing Markets* (November).

European Mortgage Federation (2006) *Study on interest rate variability in Europe* (July).

Instituto Nacional de Estadística (INE) (www.ine.es).

International Monetary Fund, *World Economic Outlook Database* (http://www.imf.org/external/pubs/ft/weo/2008/01/weodata/index.aspx).

'La Caixa' Research Department, *El crecimiento del mercado hipotecario europeo.*

Mercer Oliver Wyman (2003) *Study on the Financial Integration of European Mortgage Markets* (September).

Mortgage Bankers Association National Delinquency Survey (www.mbaa.org).

Mortgage Bankers Association, *Mortgage Finance Market* (www.mbaa.org).

Soley, J. and Baldé, J. 'El crédito hipotecario', IESE Business School Technical Note.

Suárez, J. L. and Vassallo, A. (2004) 'European Mortgage Market: An Overview 1992–2003', IESE Business School Working Paper WP-562 (June).

6
Financial Institutions' Funding for Mortgage Lending Purposes

While the funding activities of financial institutions have always been vitally important, they have become even more important in recent years because of the strong growth in lending activity by banks and other institutions involved in the mortgage markets. This growth forced credit institutions to find the necessary funding, leading them to draw on new sources of funds and develop others that had only been marginal in the past. Some funding instruments that have become particularly significant are mortgage bonds, and, in particular, structured mortgage products such as mortgage-backed securities (MBS). Derivatives related to these mortgage funding instruments have also become very important, including collateralized debt obligations (CDO) and credit default swaps (CDS), among others. (This chapter includes concepts and data from Suárez and Vassallo, 2004.)

In 2005, 66 per cent of credit institution funding came from retail deposits, 20 per cent from covered bonds (representing 50 per cent mortgage bonds; 46 per cent covered bonds to fund public-sector lending; 3 per cent covered bonds backed by ship loans; and 3 per cent backed by mixed assets), and 5 per cent from mortgage-backed securities; see Figure 6.1. Other forms of funding for mortgages may include reliance on wholesale markets, insurance revenue, short-term liquidity from warehouse lenders, contract saving schemes or mortgage portfolio sales and so on. MBS have grown considerably in importance since 1998, particularly since the development of market securitization as an instrument to obtain new and more diversified funding. Securitization permits the lender to transfer some of the risks on to the market.

An additional advantage of the new sources of funds for credit institutions (the securities market) is that they normally convey longer terms and more fixed – or easier to fix – interest rates. Typical credit institutions attract mainly short-term funds from the public and lend them

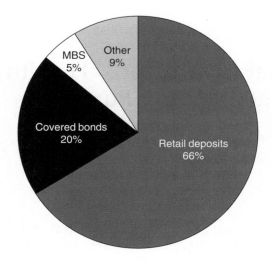

Figure 6.1   Funding of credit institutions in Europe, November 2005
Source: European Mortgage Federation, 2007.

mainly long-term, with the mortgage as security. The financial resources of credit institutions are therefore more volatile than their financial investments. This gives rise to interest rate, refinancing and opportunity risks, which the credit institution passes on to borrowers by increasing the cost of credit and the variability of interest rates. If credit institutions could attract long-term funds mobilizing the assets on their balance sheet (that is, their mortgage portfolios) by issuing securities guaranteed by those portfolios, then they could eliminate or mitigate those risks. They would presumably also be able to grant more mortgage loans at lower cost.

Another factor that has fuelled the growth of new sources of funds has been the required return of credit institutions. The institutions' revenues are sensitive to interest rates; a decrease in interest rates may mean less income for the same volume of loans. Consequently, to maintain the overall return, the volume must be increased. The lending market that has enabled financial institutions to achieve faster growth – until mid-2007 – has been the mortgage market. Mortgage loans have also had the added appeal of representing an asset that has facilitated funding through securitization. In the process, in addition to generating financial resources, the institutions have benefited from the spread between the original loans and the coupons paid to the holders of the fixed-income securities (structured mortgage products) formed from the securitization of mortgage pools. It is suspected that the enormous appeal of the asset underlying the mortgage loans has encouraged a certain laxness in the quality controls performed at origination.

Of the financing sources mentioned, we shall deal in this chapter with mortgage bonds and mortgage-backed securities, since retail deposits are already well-known and need no further discussion here. The chapter also covers the development of structured products such as collateralized debt obligations. The recent development of the primary mortgage markets, and its funding through securities, and the depressed activity in CDOs as a result of the financial turmoil originating in mid-2007 is also presented.

Mortgage bonds

Mortgage bonds are bonds covered by mortgage loans and are a category of covered bonds, which also include bonds covered by the public-sector and by ship loans. The range of eligible cover assets is defined by national covered bond systems. A mortgage bond is a full recourse debt instrument secured by a pool of specifically-identified, eligible mortgage assets. When a mortgage lender issues mortgage bonds, it keeps both the bonds and the loans on its balance sheet; that is, mortgage bonds are an on-balance-sheet instrument.

The level of security offered to mortgage bondholders enables credit institutions to raise funds from the capital markets at lower cost. Mortgage bonds are based on the credit institution's mortgage loans, which are used as collateral for the issuance of securities on the capital markets. The issuing credit institution bears the credit risk of the bonds. From the investor's point of view, mortgage bonds have the same credit risk as the credit institution itself, and represent a claim on the underlying mortgages. They are also subject to a strict legal framework. In the event of bankruptcy, there are legal provisions covering the asset pools created for the purpose of bond issuance, apart from the collateral assets that are exclusive to those pools, ensuring the cash flow stream for bondholders and timely payment.

In some countries, the law defines which loans are eligible as collateral and when this is the case they are often kept in a separate pool, while in other countries all the mortgages or all the balance sheet assets serve as collateral for the bonds (see the European Mortgage Federation References). Despite selling the loans, the originating institution usually continues to service them, which involves collecting principal and interest payments and performing other tasks.

The volume outstanding of covered bonds at the end of 2006 amounted to over 950 billion euros. The most important issuing

Table 6.1   Mortgage bonds outstanding, selected
European countries, 2006 (millions of euros)

Denmark	300,367
Germany	223,306
Spain	214,768
Sweden	55,208
United Kingdom	50,594
France	43,012
Switzerland	23,096
Republic of Ireland	11,900
Netherlands	7,500
Austria	3,420
Finland	3,000

Sources: ECBC and EMF, 2007.

countries are Denmark, Germany and Spain (ECBC and EMF, 2007).
The first three of these countries had an outstanding balance of more
than 300 billion euros worth of mortgage bonds at the end of 2006, as
shown in Table 6.1.

Denmark is the European leader in mortgage bonds, with a volume
of more than 300 billion euros in 2006, 55 per cent higher than in
2001 (The facts and data quoted below are from the *"European Covered
Bond Fact Book"*, European Covered Bond Council (ECBC), 2007 Edi-
tion). In Denmark, only mortgage specialist banks are allowed to issue
Realkreditobligationer; in practice, eight mortgage banks cover nearly
100 per cent of the Danish mortgage market. Danish mortgage bonds
account for 31.4 per cent of all European mortgage bonds outstanding;
see Figure 6.2.

Germany had the largest value of mortgage bonds outstanding in
Europe until 2004, when Denmark overtook them. Germany has not
had a major increase in mortgage bonds outstanding since 1997, and
they even started to decrease in 2001: the volume of bonds outstanding
issued by mortgage banks between 2003 and 2006 fell by 39 per cent.
Germany represents 23.4 per cent of the European mortgage bond
market. The types of mortgage bonds known as *Hypothekenpfandbriefe*,
and public mortgage bonds (*öffentliche Pfandbriefe*), totalled 944 billion
euros, with mortgage bonds accounting for 20 per cent of this volume.
The *Jumbo Pfandbriefe* amounted to 345 billion euros.

In 2002, the mortgage bonds outstanding in Spain amounted to 25
billion euros, representing 4 per cent of the European total, and then

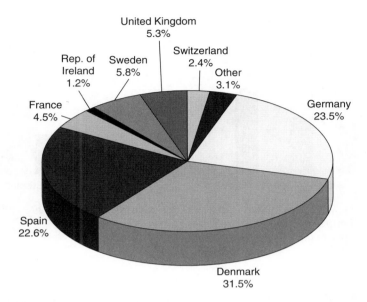

Figure 6.2 European mortgage bonds outstanding, 2006 (countries' share by volume; percentages)

Note: The category 'Other' comprises Austria, the Netherlands, Hungary, Czech Republic, Finland, Portugal, Slovakia, Poland, Latvia, Lithuania, Italy (Cassa Depositi e Prestiti) and Luxembourg.

Sources: ECBC and EMF, 2007.

grew further in 2006 to 22.5 per cent, ranked as the third-largest volume outstanding in Europe. In 2006, 33 per cent of mortgage loans were financed by mortgage bonds, up from only 7 per cent in 2002. After taxation rules changed in 1999, the Spanish mortgage bond market experienced a healthy growth, reaching 215 billion euros at the end of 2006 In Spain, any credit institution regulated by the Bank of Spain is allowed to issue mortgage bonds.

Denmark and Spain are the only countries with a reported increase in mortgage bonds outstanding; in other countries the balances have remained stable or decreased. The evolution of the mortgage bonds was independent of the previous level of development in the case of both these countries: Denmark already had a large balance in 1996, while Spain had only a small one at that time. This also applies to other countries, as can be seen in Figure 6.3, which portrays the evolution of mature markets, and Figure 6.4, showing the evolution of markets that were less developed in 1996. The changes in the markets may be related to the huge development of mortgage markets in Denmark and Spain, and with the increased importance and attractiveness of the MBS.

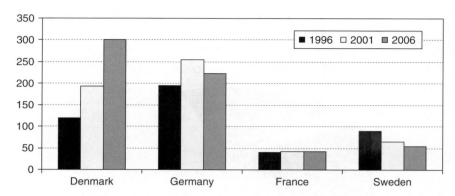

Figure 6.3 Mortgage bonds outstanding: mature markets, 1996–2006 (in billions of euros)
Source: European Mortgage Federation (2007).

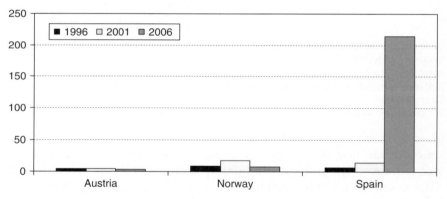

Figure 6.4   Mortgage bonds outstanding: less developed markets, 1996–2006 (in billions of euros)
Source: European Mortgage Federation (2007).

Swedish funding through bonds increased before 2005, as a result of the popularity of fixed-rate loans, which are usually bond-funded. They are still the most popular funding method in Sweden. Outstanding loans provided by mortgage institutions increased by 9.1 per cent during 2006. Sweden was in fourth place in 2006, with a balance of mortgage bonds outstanding of 55 billion euros, representing 5.8 per cent of the European total. It should be remembered that the Swedish Covered Bond Act came into force in 2006. The bonds issued before 2006 are not fully comparable with the bonds in use since then. In spite of this, the figures are included in Figure 6.3. Mortgage bonds issued in Sweden before 2006, known as *Hypoteksbanksobligationer*, were not subject to special regulation and were not collateralized directly. Instead, they were covered by the bank's entire balance sheet, and the privileged position of the bond holder was enhanced by the strict limitation of the mortgage institution's assets to mortgage lending. A large part of the mortgage bonds stock was converted into covered bonds in 2006. The outstanding balance in 2006 of Swedish mortgage-backed covered bonds is shown in Table 6.1, and Figure 6.3 includes both the converted bonds and the new bonds issued during the year. Around 70 per cent of the funding obtained by Swedish credit institutions is obtained via the issuance of mortgage bonds.

After Sweden comes the United Kingdom, with more than 50 billion euros, representing 5.3 per cent of the European total. Following the launch of the first covered bond by HBOS in 2003, the market has developed rapidly, but the regulatory environment for covered bonds has struggled to keep pace. In contrast to other European countries, the United Kingdom has no specific legislation, and issues are governed by contract law. However, this is changing – on 23 July 2007, the UK Treasury and the UK Financial Services Authority (FSA) published a joint consultation document entitled *Proposals for a UK Recognized Covered Bonds Legislative Framework*. The consultation paper sets out draft legislation which is scheduled to come into force on 1 January 2008.

In France, mortgage bonds outstanding decreased year on year from 2003 to 2005, but then in 2006 rallied and returned to the 2002 position of 40 billion euros. The issuances increased by 100 per cent in 2006, raising the total volume of bonds outstanding by 34 per cent. At the end of 2006, the volume of mortgage bonds outstanding was 43 billion euros, representing 4.5 per cent of the European total, making France the sixth-largest market in Europe. Since the inception of the French Mortgage Act in 1999, French *Obligations Foncières* have been issued by specialist credit institutions (*Sociétés de Crédit Foncier* – SCFs) and are collateralized by mortgage and public-sector loans, which together constitute a single cover pool. SCFs are designed as funding vehicles (typically without staff) and are usually managed by another credit institution, generally the holding parent bank. They do not usually run asset origination on their own. According to Hypostat (European Mortgage Federation), in 2002 mortgage bonds funded around 6.5 per cent of residential mortgage loans.

The seventh-largest market is Switzerland, with 23 billion euros of mortgage loans outstanding. The main distinguishing feature of the Swiss market with respect to the rest of Europe is that it has no mortgage banks, but instead has two institutions known as *Pfandbriefzentrale*, which finance their member institutions (public and private commercial banks) by issuing *Pfandbriefe*.

In Austria, 6.6 per cent of mortgage loans are financed by mortgage bonds. Among the 17 billion euros of Austrian covered bonds, mortgage bonds outstanding at the end of 2006 amounted to 3.4 billion euros. Other covered bonds are backed by the public sector, accounting for 80 per cent of the total. Under Austrian law, banks can issue two kinds of covered bonds: *Pfandbriefe*, which are issued under the Mortgage Banking Act and Mortgage Bond Act; and *Fundierte Bankschuldverschreibungen* (FBS), issued under the Law on Secured Bank Bonds.

As the main objective of mortgage bonds is to finance mortgage loans, the relationship between the two is relevant. The data varied considerably from one country to another between 2000 and 2006: the proportion of mortgage bond funding increased in Spain (from 6.1 per cent to 37.6 per cent); and decreased in Sweden (from 63.1 per cent to 31.8 per cent, as a result of the enactment of the Swedish Covered Bond Act), Denmark (from 127.1 per cent to 100 per cent), France (from 15.6 per cent to 7.4 per cent), Germany (from 22.5 per cent to 18.9 per cent) and Austria (from 8 per cent to 5.6 per cent); while in the Netherlands it remained at a very low level – see Figure 6.5.

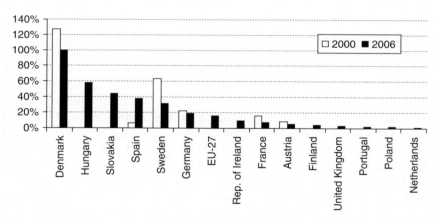

Figure 6.5   Mortgage bonds outstanding and residential mortgage loans, 2000 and 2006 (mortgage bonds/residential mortgage loans; percentages)
Note: Two observations help to consider the relationship between mortgage bonds and the mortgage loans: (i) The issue prices of the bonds are below the nominal value; and (ii) While, there is no distinction between residential or commercial lending in the mortgage bonds, only mortgage loans for residential purposes are considered.
Sources: ECBC and EMF(2007) and European Mortgage Federation (2007).

Mortgage bond issuance

Denmark and Spain stand out again in mortgage bond issuance in 2006. What was seen in the previous section for outstanding balance is repeated with the issuance market. There has been no significant growth for the other countries in volume terms in recent years. See Table 6.2.

Annual growth in mortgage bond issuance was extremely high in the Netherlands in 2006, at 175 per cent. However, the issuance level and outstanding balance are small compared with the country's mortgage market; see Figure 6.6. Finland is second to the Netherlands in issuance growth, with a compound annual growth rate over the period 2004–6 of 145 per cent; in 2006, mortgage bond issuance attained a volume of 1.5 billion euros. In the period 2003–6, the compound annual growth rate for Spain, France and Denmark are lower, but still significant. Over the same period, Germany shows a compound annual growth rate of −15 per cent between 2003 and 2006, even though it has the second-longest-standing mortgage bond market in Europe. This finding is in line with the evolution described earlier for the mortgage market as a whole, and the overall economic situation in Germany during this period.

By 2000, the mortgage bonds had already achieved the relative weight as a source of funding that they have at the time of writing. This suggests that it was not mainly mortgage bonds that fuelled the primary mortgage expansion, but rather the structured mortgage products, in particular the MBS and its derivatives, the CDOs, which progressively

Table 6.2 Mortgage bonds issued, selected European countries (in millions of euros)

Country	1992	1997	2002	2006
Denmark	11,704	33,926	76,063	114,014
Germany	21,904	41,596	40,857	35,336
Spain	1,433	2,194	n.a.	69,890
France	5,305	302	17,000	12,637
Netherlands	159	296	5	5,500
Austria	719	681	268	n.a.
Finland	251	349	n.a.	1,500
Sweden	19,982	24,027	25,590	17,550
Norway	1,7094	731	2,311	n.a.

Source: European Mortgage Federation (2007).

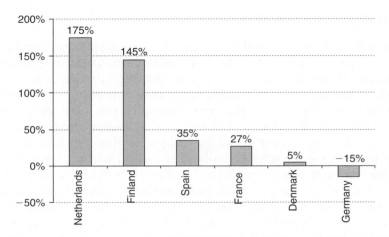

Figure 6.6   Growth in mortgage bond issuance, 2003–6 (compound annual growth rate; percentages)
Note: The rate of growth for the Netherlands is calculated from 2005; and in Finland from 2004.
Source: European Mortgage Federation (2007).

gained relative weight as sources of funds for financial institutions during this period. The volume acquired by these products during the period of mortgage growth will be discussed below.

The behaviour of the mortgage bonds market during 2007 paralleled the evolution of the financial markets in general. The slowdown in mortgage origination and the lack of confidence on the interbank market led to falls in mortgage bond issuance in Europe. By way of example, the charts below show these issues' behaviour in Germany and Spain; see Figure 6.7.

After recording a growth rate of 5 per cent in 2006, the German issues fell by 22 per cent in 2007. In Spain, growth has been much greater in recent years (38.3 per cent in 2006), but the fall in 2007 for the period with data available (January to September) was also much sharper, 40 per cent less than the same period in 2006.

Mortgage-backed securities

When a credit institution issues mortgage-backed securities, it isolates the receivables and their associated cash flows from its other assets by selling them to a special purpose vehicle (SPV), which then issues the securities. The cash flows generated by the assets can be used to make payments on the securities issued to investors. In the securitization

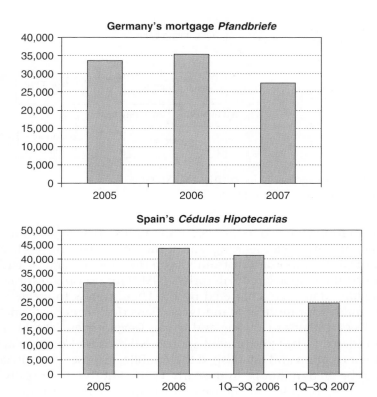

Figure 6.7 Mortgage bond issue, Germany and Spain, 2006 and 2007 (in millions of euros)
Sources: Association of German Pfandbriefe Banks and Asociación Hipotecaria Española.

process, cash flow streams coming from loans are converted into marketable securities. Depending on whether the mortgages are residential or commercial, the SPV will issue residential mortgage-backed securities (RMBS) or commercial mortgage-backed securities (CMBS) (European Mortgage Federation).

Independent rating agencies evaluate the credit quality and integrity of the securitization structure. Note that the payment flows from the loans may be uncertain, as there is the possibility of delinquency, whereas the payment flows to investors are considered to be more certain. This is why each issue is subject to an examination to detect any possibility of non-payment by borrowers, so that any anticipated difficulty in making payments to investors can be resolved. Sometimes this involves buying an insurance policy; see Figure 6.8.

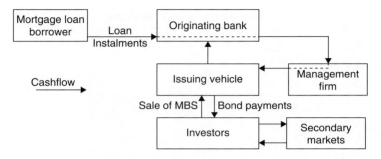

Figure 6.8   Mortgage-backed securities (MBS) issue
Source: Suárez, Ortega and García (1998).

Securitization emerged in the USA in the 1970s as a means of stimulating residential mortgage lending, and at the time of writing has become one of the most important instruments on the capital markets. The first two government-sponsored enterprises (GSEs) for housing, Fannie Mae and Freddie Mac, were chartered by the US Congress to create a secondary market for residential mortgage loans (for further information, see US Department of Housing and Urban Development, 2008). These are considered to be 'government-sponsored' because Congress authorized their creation and established their public purposes. Securitization began to be used in Europe in the early 1990s, but it did not really take off until 1997 or 1998. At the time of writing, credit institutions in a number of EU countries, and above all in the USA, obtain finance by issuing MBS.

MBS are structured mortgage products that have gained greater importance in recent years. Several factors have enabled this to happen: the increase in funding requirements of financial institutions to support the huge growth in mortgage lending; the regulatory pressure of Basel II on the credit risk assumed by financial institutions (stimulating them to remove a pool of mortgages from the balance sheet); the availability of credit enhancement mechanisms; and good marks from rating agencies. The latter boosted the ease of selling the securities.

Among the more active countries in the mortgage-backed securities market are the United Kingdom, Spain, the Netherlands, France, the Republic of Ireland and Italy. In recent years there has been faster growth in Spain, the Netherlands, the Republic of Ireland and the United Kingdom.

The United Kingdom has the largest MBS market in Europe but, unfortunately, there is no data for this country before 2006. In the third quarter of 2007 the outstanding MBS of the United Kingdom represented

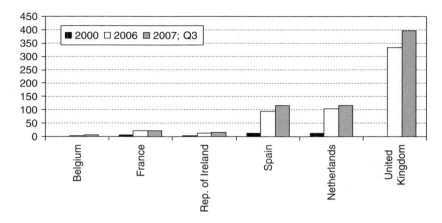

Figure 6.9 MBS outstanding, 2000–7 (in billions of euros)
Note: No data are available for United Kingdom in 2000.
Sources: European Mortgage Federation (2007); European Securitization Forum (2007).

57 per cent of the European market. Figure 6.9 shows rapid growth in all countries, but especially in Spain and the Netherlands, where growth over the period 2000–6 was about 100 billion euros in each country.

In 2006, in Europe as a whole, the volume of issues hit a record high, reaching 474.5 billion euros. Particularly interesting is that, looking at quarterly results, we see the last quarter of 2006 saw sales of 185.8 billion euros, more than 63 per cent greater than the previous quarter (113.5 billion), and 29.5 per cent greater than in the same quarter of the previous year. This dramatic growth is a result of the search for assets that offered higher returns without excessive perceived risk. At the same time, the outlook for companies' financial health and credit quality favoured the growth of the securitization market, which has become a major driver in the economy, with annual growth of around 60 per cent.

The United Kingdom is the largest player in issuance, with an annual average of MBS of more than 86 billion euros in the period of 2003–06. Spain and the Netherlands are next, with a big gap before the remaining European countries; see Table 6.3.

The strong position of the United Kingdom in MBS issuance is mirrored in its 51 per cent market share in 2006; see Figure 6.10. Spain is second with 12 per cent, representing issues worth 44 billion euros. Close behind Spain is Germany, with a 10 per cent market share, then Italy and the Netherlands, each with 8 per cent.

In the 2000s, the strongest growth in MBS issuance was in Greece (albeit with a very low absolute level) followed by Spain. In general,

Table 6.3   Residential mortgage-backed securities issued, selected European countries, 1996–2006 (average annual issuance in each period; in millions of euros)

	1996–99	2000–02	2003–06
United Kingdom		27,799	86,311
Spain	2,654	6,072	24,982
Netherlands	1,589	11,404	21,365
Italy		7,323	7,433
Portugal		1,450	6,080
France		4,590	4,923
Republic of Ireland	637	1,713	4,507
Germany		3,030	2,823
Greece			1,523

Source: European Mortgage Federation (2007).

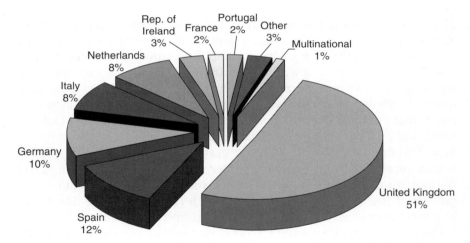

Figure 6.10   European securitization issuance market, 2006 (countries' percentage shares)
Source: European Securitization Forum (2007) *Data Report* (Summer).

all countries with a high level of expansion of the mortgage market, or with a consolidated, mature mortgage market, have shown significant growth; see Figure 6.11. Growth was continuous during the period studied and has been linked to the steady development of the real estate market in these countries, and the increase in the volume of mortgages.

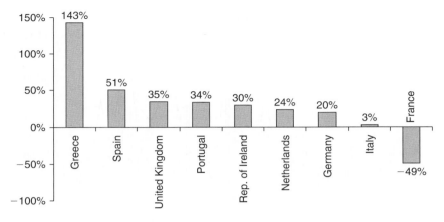

Figure 6.11 Growth in MBS issuance, 2000–6 (compound percentage annual growth rate)
Note: Data not available for certain countries: France, 2000, 2001; Republic of Ireland, 2004; Germany, 2000, 2001; Greece, 2000, 2001, 2002; Portugal, 2000.
Source: European Mortgage Federation (2007).

Credit institutions have found securitization to be an efficient way of raising funds and developing their businesses. As was seen earlier, the growth in MBS issuance has generally been greater than the annual growth of gross mortgage lending, reflecting the weight gained by the MBS as a means of funding lending institutions.

Behind Spain are the United Kingdom, Portugal, the Republic of Ireland and the Netherlands – the latter having seen steady growth in securitization since 1996. France is the only country among those studied to show a reduction in the issue of MBS (note that the historic data for this country only starts from 2002).

In the first half of 2007, Spain issued 31 billion euros of MBS, a 64 per cent increase on the first half of 2006, while the United Kingdom issued 124 billion euros in the first half of the year, 84 per cent up on the same period in 2006. This reflects the strong growth of securitization up to June 2007, driven primarily by MBS (in both forms, RMBS and CMBS) and by CDOs (see next section), which represented 85 per cent of European securitization issuance in 2006.

MBS issuance has stopped completely since the summer of 2007, when the subprime mortgage crisis in the USA began to affect the international financial system. CMBS issues in the second half of 2007 have recorded year-on-year rates of variation of between −50 per cent and −80 per cent; see Figure 6.12. Of the non-US issues made in 2007, 23.1 per cent were

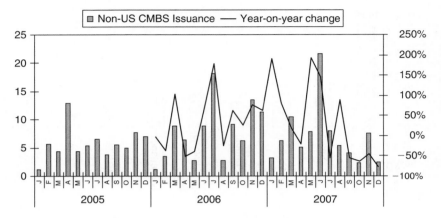

Figure 6.12   Non-US CMBS issuance, 2005–7 (in billions of dollars)
Source: Commercial Mortgage Alert (accessed March 2008).

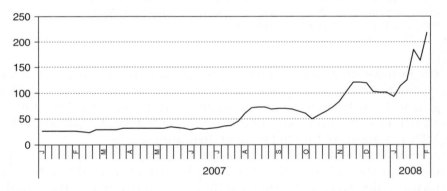

Figure 6.13   CMBS spreads, 2007–8 (10-year CMBS AAA spread over swaps; in basis points)
Note: AAA refers to the best category awarded by rating agencies. In relation to securities, it always corresponds to senior tranches.
Source: Commercial Mortgage Alert (accessed March 2008).

made in the United Kingdom, 51.1 per cent in other European countries, 17.8 per cent in Japan and 7.2 per cent in other countries.

The difficulty in placing the CMBS can also be seen in the strong growth in the spreads demanded to invest in these securities; see Figure 6.13. Apart from decreasing the role played by MBS in lending institutions' funding (a restriction on funding that has meant fewer funds available to institutions, to finance their customers), it also affects the value of the securities that many investors, including banks and their subsidiaries, include in their asset portfolios.

In the USA, the CMBS issuance volume up to June 2007 was enormous. After September, the year-on-year variations fell below −50 per cent and, from September 2007 onwards, the monthly issuance volume in the USA equalled the volume in the rest of the world, when, traditionally, the level of issuance in the USA had been much higher; see Figure 6.14.

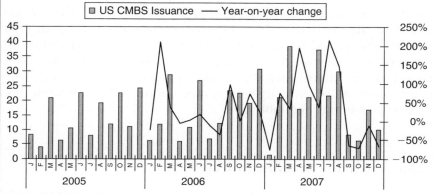

Figure 6.14   US CMBS issuance, 2005–7 (in billions US dollars)
Source: Commercial Mortgage Alert (accessed March 2008).

As noted previously, on occasion securities, loans and derivatives are insured in order to enhance their quality. The largest insurers participating in this process are American firms sometimes called 'monolines' that carried an AAA rating themselves, and this rating is transferred to the derivatives insured. The delinquency rate in mortgages in the second half of 2007 and early 2008, mainly subprime loans granted in America, caused the rating agencies to place the rating of insurers into observation, with the danger of a downgrading. If that were to happen, the value of MBS and CDO would decrease, putting more pressure on the balance sheets of investors worldwide. It is estimated that these firms have insured securities valued at around 125 billion US dollars.

Mortgage bonds versus mortgage-backed securities

Mortgage bonds differ from MBS in that the loans are not transferred; instead, the originating institution itself sets up the fund and issues the securities. On the one hand, the resulting securities have a strong guarantee because, in any event, as well as the collateral assets, they are also covered by the originator's other assets. This has a downside, however, in that the bonds are also subject to the originator's business risk. With mortgage bonds, the credit institution retains responsibility for the bond's credit risk until maturity, as well as for prepayment risk, which means that the risk assumed by the investor is small (market risk only).

MBS are different with respect to risk. On the one hand, they are not subject to the originator's business risk, as they are held by an independent entity; and on the other, because the originating institution transfers the credit risk, the early repayment risk and the market risk to the SPV along with the loans themselves, these risks are assumed by the investor, who will eventually require much higher rates of interest than on mortgage bonds; see Table 6.4.

Collateralized debt obligations (CDOs)

In the case of mortgages, the funding chain has gone beyond the MBS. During the 1980s, collateralized debt obligations, CDOs began to be traded (Fabozzi and Choudhry, 2004). The CDOs appeared as a generic name derived from the Collateralized Mortgage Obligations (CMOs), which existed in the USA. CDOs vary in structure and underlying collateral, but the basic principle is the same. First, a CDO entity acquires an inventory of securities – such as MBS. Then, the CDO entity sells rights to the cash flows from the inventory, along with their associated risk. The sold rights are called tranches in accordance with the cash flow and risk assignment rules of the CDO: senior (rated AAA) tranches are paid first followed by mezzanine (AA to BB) tranches, and equity tranches (unrated).

CDOs offer exposure to the credit of a portfolio of fixed income assets and divide the credit risk among different tranches. The types of collateral for cash CDOs include:

- structured finance securities (RMBS and CMBS);
- leveraged loans;
- corporate bonds;
- REITs' debts (unsecuritized commercial real estate loans);
- emerging-market sovereign debt; and
- project finances' debt.

Table 6.4 Differences between mortgage bonds and mortgage-backed securities

Criteria	Mortgage bonds	Mortgage-backed securities
Mortgage bond production	Bundled process	Unbundled process
Type of securitization (balance sheet treatment)	Assets remain on the balance sheet of the originating institution ('on-balance-sheet securitization')	Generally, assets are removed from the balance sheet of the originating institution ('off-balance-sheet securitization')
Source of principal and interest payments	Issuer cash flow	Collateral cash flow
Risk exposure:		
Credit risk	Issuer	Investor
Prepayment risk	Issuer	Investor
Market risk	Investor	Investor
Investor protection in event of issuer bankruptcy	Bankruptcy privilege: The bondholder has a priority claim on assets in the event that the issuer becomes bankrupt (quasi-bankruptcy remoteness)	Bankruptcy remoteness is built into the structure of the MBS (bankruptcy of the originating institution does not affect the servicing of the MBS)
Credit quality	In addition to the asset quality, it depends mainly on the strength of the originating institution and the legal framework	In addition to the asset quality, it depends mainly on the strength of the structure created

(*Continued*)

Table 6.4 (Continued)

Criteria	Mortgage bonds	Mortgage-backed securities
Over-collateralization	Defined by law	Usually required for a high credit rating
Tiered capital	Subordination is inherent in the system (e.g. requirement to respect certain LTV ratios)	A structure distinguishing structure between senior and subordinating securities needs to be created
Guarantee	A guarantee (if given) will be provided by the originating mortgage credit institution	Guarantee provided by a third party such as an insurance company or bank ('credit enhancement')
Collateral pool	1. Individual components of the asset pool are substitutable 2. Mainly heterogeneous assets 3. Eligible assets defined by law LTV ratios and sound property valuation methods)	1. Individual components of structure the asset pool are (in general) not substitutable 2. Mainly homogeneous assets 3. Eligible assets are not necessarily defined by law
Interest payment	Typically yearly	Typically monthly
Principal redemption	Bullet form	Amortization and prepayments

Source: European Mortgage Federation (2004).

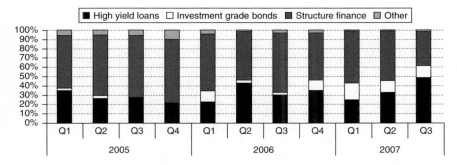

Figure 6.15   Types of collateral in CDO issuance, 2005–7 (percentages)
Source: Securities Industry and Financial Markets Association (SIFMA) (2008).

The most illiquid, highest-risk assets tend to predominate among the collaterals for CDOs; see Figure 6.15.

The pooling concept that a CDO provides can attract scalable liquidity to an asset class. The high-yield market serves as a good example here; without the capacity made available to high-yield issuers through CDOs, the market would not have been able to develop as rapidly as it did in terms of size and breadth. It is estimated that, globally, approximately two-thirds of all US high-yield new issuance is intermediated to end-investors through CDOs.

Since the 1990s, CDOs have been the fastest-growing asset class in the asset-backed securities market. The 1990s were a period where complexity in financial markets increased significantly as a result of the globalization of investable opportunities. Many credit markets have come of age since then: European, Asian and other emerging markets. However, the volume increased most significantly during the first years of the 2000s; see Figure 6.16. The situation changed dramatically after 9 August 2007 – when BNP Paribas revealed large unanticipated losses on US subprime securities. The 60 per cent drop in issues in the third quarter of 2007 reflects the loss of confidence in this type of structured product as a consequence of the subprime mortgages – mainly from the USA – embedded in the CDOs.

The CDO investors cover a wide range of institutions that intend to diversify their portfolios and to take advantage of the ease of taking positions in the different kinds of financial assets they offer and the apparently favourable risk–return trade-off. As can be seen from Figure 6.17, most CDOs outstanding are in the banks' portfolios, while other important investors are asset managers, insurance companies and pension funds.

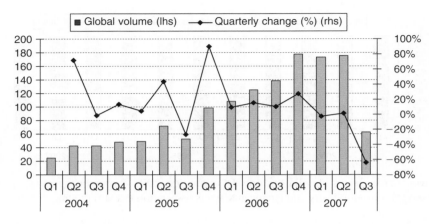

Figure 6.16   Global CDO issuance, 2004–7 (global volume, in billions of dollars and percentage of quarterly change)
Source: Securities Industry and Financial Markets Association (SIFMA) (2008).

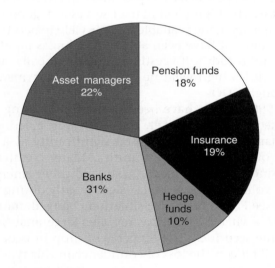

Figure 6.17   CDO holders, 2007
Source: International Monetary Fund (November 2007).

The CDOs described so far have been cash flow CDOs, which are structured to pay off liabilities with the interest and principal payments (cash flows) of their collateral. In addition to these, there are synthetic CDOs. Synthetic CDOs sell credit protection via credit default swaps (CDSs) rather than by purchasing cash assets. Synthetic CDOs use CDSs to replicate a cash flow CDO synthetically. Funded tranches require the deposit of cash into an SPV at the inception of the deal to collateralize portions of the SPV's potential swap obligations in the transaction; losses result in principal write-downs of the issued notes.

Large parts of the CDOs are in the hands of structured investment vehicles (SIVs) – ad hoc vehicles that fund the CDOs, mainly in the short-term securities markets, through commercial paper or medium-term notes (MTN). These SIVs are sponsored by banks, and other institutional investors such as insurance companies and private equity funds. Since the summer of 2007, the activities of SIVs have faced two large and embarrassing distortions – one is the dramatic illiquidity of most security markets; and the other is related to the quality of their assets. The loss in value in the subjacent assets of the CDOs, and of the CDOs themselves, forced the sponsoring institutions either to increase their equity in the SIVs, or to merge them into their own balance sheets, or to let them fall into default. Until the early months of 2008, large banks were obliged to write-down around 120 billion dollars, and other institutions were bailed out, such as the US investment bank, Bear Stearns.

CDOs in euros

Multinational issuers predominate in the CDOs issued in euros, whose volume reached 273.2 billion euros of stock outstanding in the third quarter of 2006. In fact, the stock outstanding associated with multinational issuers exceeds that of the all the European countries put together.

In terms of individual European countries, Spain is the indisputable leader, with 39.3 billion euros of stock outstanding in the third quarter of 2007; see Table 6.5. This situation has been encouraged by two basic factors: the impressive growth in residential building; and the expansion in mortgages. Spain is followed by Germany, which also has a significant CDO market, with 18.7 billion euros of stock outstanding in the third quarter of 2007.

The Netherlands is in third place, with 10.5 billion euros of CDOs outstanding and a growth rate of 43.8 per cent as at December 2006. This was also caused by the lending expansion that took place in the Netherlands in the early 2000s, and the resulting need to find new forms of funding, reflected in the figures for MBS and CDO issues. The growth in 2007 in the United Kingdom is particularly striking – an impressive 245.5 per cent.

Table 6.5   Country breakdown of CDOs issued in euros, selected European countries (outstanding volume in billions of euros)

	Market outstanding volume		Percentage Change
	December 2006	**Q3 2007**	
Denmark		6.5	
France	0.6	0.9	50.0
Germany	14.4	18.7	29.9
Greece	2.3	2.3	0.0
Republic of Ireland	2.0	2.0	0.0
Italy	4.4	5.4	22.7
Netherlands	7.3	10.5	43.8
Portugal	1.8	1.5	−16.7
Russia		0.2	
Spain	37.9	39.3	3.7
Switzerland		0.4	
United Kingdom	2.2	7.6	245.5
Multinational	148.0	177.9	20.2

Source: European Securitization Forum (2007) *Data Report* (Autumn).

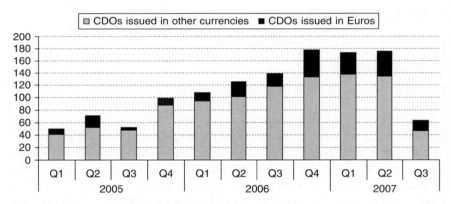

Figure 6.18   Currency breakdown of CDO issuance, 2005–7 (in billions of US dollars)
Source: Securities Industry and Financial Markets Association (SIFMA) (2008).

While the volume of CDO issues in euros has become increasingly important in recent years, issues in US dollars are still the most common; see Figure 6.18. CDO issues in euros fell by 60.3 per cent in the third quarter of 2007 compared with the second quarter of the same year.

Harmonization initiatives in the European secondary mortgage markets

In the secondary mortgage market a number of initiatives have also been undertaken, aimed at harmonizing the regulations affecting commercial banks when they decide to issue mortgage-collateralized bonds. These initiatives have originated from both public and private sources. The former include the UCITS Directive and the Capital Requirements Directive, based on Basel II, while the European Mortgage Finance Agency (EMFA) was a private initiative.

The 1998 Undertaking for the Collective Investment of Transferable Securities Directive (UCITS) sets out a number of criteria that mortgage bonds must meet (European Mortgage Federation, 2008):

- They must be issued by credit institutions, and in accordance with legal provisions, to protect bondholders.
- They are subject to special supervision by public authorities.
- The sums deriving from issuance of mortgage bonds must be placed in assets that provide sufficient cover for the liabilities deriving from the bonds until maturity.
- In the event of bankruptcy of the issuer, sums deriving from the issuance of mortgage bonds must be used as a priority to repay principal and interest becoming due.
- Issues must be notified to the European Commission.

Another cornerstone of covered bond regulation at EU level is the recent Capital Requirement Directive (CRD). Basel II has been implemented in the European Union via the CRD. Transposition of the CRD corresponds to the national authorities. The Committee of European Banking Supervision (CEBS) gives advice to the European Commission on banking policy issues, and promotes co-operation and convergence of supervisory practice across the European Union. The Committee will endeavour where possible to limit or harmonize the areas where national discretion can be applied. The CRD rules will apply to all credit institutions and investment service providers in the EU, revising the supervisory regulations governing the capital adequacy of internationally active banks.

The European Council formally adopted the CRD on 7 June 2006. The implementation of the CRD at national level is to take place between that date and enactment in 2008. As covered bonds play an important role in EU financial markets, the EU Commission has decided to establish a privileged treatment for them. According to the CRD, covered bonds benefit from privileged credit risk weightings only if they fulfil the following requirements:

1. Compliance with the standards of the UCITS Directive.
2. The asset pools that back the covered bonds must be constituted only of assets of specifically defined types and credit quality.
3. New quantitative restrictions on certain types of cover assets were established (for example, maximum 15 per cent exposure to credit institutions).
4. The issuers of covered bonds backed by mortgage loans must meet certain minimum requirements regarding mortgage property valuation and monitoring.

Only if these requirements are transposed by each EU member state can privileged treatment of covered bonds be obtained or maintained. While the UCITS Directive provided a fairly general and abstract framework, the CRD framework is much more specific in its definition of covered bonds (ECBC and EMF, 2007).

An initiative from the private sector dated November 2003 was the creation of the European Mortgage Finance Agency (EMFA), based on Freddie Mac and Fannie Mae – two of the largest US financial institutions, which make a unified, liquid and publicly-backed secondary market in mortgage securities. The EMFA was set up by the following institutions to create a single, pan-European mortgage market:

- BBVA, Spain;
- Crédit Agricole, France;
- Banco Comercial Portugués (BCP), Portugal;
- Northern Rock, United Kingdom – bailed out by the British government in 2007; and
- Irish Life and Permanent, Republic of Ireland.

The project eventually failed (Nasarre Aznar, 2007). The aim in setting up the EMFA was to create a single mortgage securitization market from which lenders would be able to obtain funds to finance new and better-quality loans on better terms. This would be achieved through the standardization of products, processes and guarantee systems.

Another goal of the EMFA was to promote long-term, fixed-rate loans without prepayment fees, which would be much safer than the variable-rate loans subject to constant changes in interest rates that previously predominated in Spain and the United Kingdom in particular. The new market would be funded by private capital but could have the backing of the EU.

Bibliography

Asociación Hipotecaria Española, *Estadística de Títulos Hipotecarios* (www.ahe.es).

Commercial Mortgage Alert (www.CMAlert.com). Accessed March 2008.

ECBC and EMF (European Covered Bond Council and European Mortgage Federation) (2007) *European Covered Bond Fact Book* (August).

European Mortgage Federation (2007) *Hypostat 2006: A review of Europe's Mortgage and Housing Markets* (November).

European Mortgage Federation (2004) *Mortgage Bonds vs. Mortgage Backed Securities.*

European Mortgage Federation, *The Economic and Financial Importance of Mortgage Bonds.*

European Mortgage Federation, *What Are Mortgage Bonds?*

European Securitization Forum (2007) *Data Report Autumn 2007.*

European Securitization Forum (2007) *Data Report Summer 2007.*

Fabozzi, F. J. and Choudhry, M. (2004)*Handbook of European Structured Financial Products* (John Wiley: Adobe e-book).

International Monetary Fund, *World Economic Outlook Database.*

Nasarre Aznar, S., (2007) 'Causas y evolución de la crisis hipotecaria de 2007', *Comunicación empresarial* (December).

Securities Industry and Financial Markets Association (SIFMA), *Global CDO Markets Issuance Data.*

Suárez, J. L. and Vassallo, A. (2004) 'European Mortgage Market: An Overview 1992–2003', IESE Business School Working Paper WP-562 (June).

Suarez, J. L., I. Ortega I. and García, A (1998) 'Hipotebansa III', *Case from IESE Business School.*

US Department of Housing and Urban Development (2008) *HUD's Regulation of Fannie Mae and Freddie Mac.*

Index

Key: **bold** = extended discussion; b = box; f = figure; n = note; t = table.